C000152644

Withdrawn from
Lambeth Libraries

RUPERT'S ADVENTURES IN CHINA

Withdrawn from
Lambeth Libraries

RUPERT'S ADVENTURES IN CHINA

HOW MURDOCH LOST A FORTUNE AND FOUND A WIFE

BRUCE DOVER

MAINSTREAM
PUBLISHING

EDINBURGH AND LONDON

London Borough of Lambeth	
LM 1174257 7	
Askews	21-Nov-2008
302.23	£18.99

Copyright © Bruce Dover, 2008
All rights reserved
The moral right of the author has been asserted

First published in Great Britain in 2008 by
MAINSTREAM PUBLISHING COMPANY (EDINBURGH) LTD
7 Albany Street
Edinburgh EH1 3UG

ISBN 9781845962777

First published in Australia in 2008 by
Penguin Group (Australia)

No part of this book may be reproduced or transmitted in any form or by
any other means without permission in writing from the publisher, except
by a reviewer who wishes to quote brief passages in connection with a review
written for insertion in a magazine, newspaper or broadcast

This book is a work of non-fiction based on the life, experiences and recollections of
the author. In some cases, names of people, places, dates, sequences or
the detail of events have been changed to protect the privacy of others. The
author has stated to the publishers that, except in such respects, not affecting
the substantial accuracy of the work, the contents of this book are true

Photographs © *South China Morning Post* unless otherwise indicated

A catalogue record for this book is available
from the British Library

Typeset in Berber and Fairfield Light

Printed in Great Britain by
Clays Ltd, St Ives plc

For Hoai Bich, Linh Lan
and Hoai Linh

Author's Note

Rupert Murdoch is the most impressive of businessmen and also the most pragmatic. China is the most dynamic of economies but the most challenging for outsiders to tap. In China, Murdoch's unrelenting ambition came up against the intransigence of a regime determined to keep the media titan at bay and preserve Chinese culture from what it saw as the insidious influences of a foreign invader. With the purchase of STAR TV in 1993, Murdoch took the first steps in an extraordinary journey that would see him pit the full weight of his empire – and his personal prestige – in a decade-and-a-half-long adventure aimed at conquering China's potentially lucrative television broadcasting market.

This book is an attempt to recount the trials and tribulations of Murdoch's time in China. It is not meant to be a history text but the recollections of a privileged insider, and later interested observer, which hopefully provides some insight into Murdoch deal-making philosophy as well as the pitfalls of doing business in China – no matter how big a corporate player you may be. Along the way, the text hopefully also helps humanise Murdoch the man – while demonstrating that he is undoubtedly an agent of change and that no media landscape ever remains the same in his wake. But the recollections are personal and as such any errors, faults and inconsistencies are mine and in no way attributable to the myriad of fellow travellers who in some shape or form contributed to the writing of the book.

The book really began as a series of dinner table yarns about life in China working for Murdoch. I am indebted to Eric Beecher from Private Media Partners for encouraging me to put the stories down on paper and for introducing Bob Sessions from Penguin Australia, who believed in the project.

I also extend my gratitude to my numerous sources – from China's Ministry of Foreign Affairs, People's Daily, the State Council Information Office, CCTV and SARFT – who cannot be named for fear of jeopardising their professional careers in Communist China. I also thought it wise to protect my former colleagues at News Corporation from being directly quoted, least they be tarred by any opprobrium that might come my way as a result of detailing some of the inside workings of the organisation.

My thanks to my long-time colleague and friend Ian Macintosh, for reading the drafts and offering invaluable suggestions, to Ringo Chan for his insights into the machinations of the Chinese bureaucracy, to Ken White and Kathy Mexted for their encouragement and feedback, and to my sister Bernice, who perhaps rightly claims credit for persuading me to take up journalism as a career in the first place. Acknowledgement is also due to my editor at Penguin, Michael Nolan, whose gentle cajoling, persistence and patience enabled me to deliver the finished product – not exactly on deadline, but not too far off.

And finally to my family – Hoai Bich, Linh Lan and Hoai Linh – my eternal gratitude and love for your tolerance and forbearance, and for being there when I needed you.

Bruce Dover

Contents

Withdrawn from Lambeth Libraries

1

Obsession

Beijing's Xiushui Market, or 'Silk Street', was a bustling bazaar of some 410 stalls crammed into a narrow alley that ran off the city's main thoroughfare, Jianguomenwai Dajie, and finished down near the United States Embassy in the leafy diplomatic quarter. Normally packed with a mixture of foreigners and aspiring locals, it was rated by many as the third-biggest attraction in China, outside the Forbidden City and the Great Wall, not for aesthetic reasons but because Silk Street was a haven for counterfeit luxury brand-name goods.

Here one could find the finest knock-off copies of all the world's most exclusive brands – Prada, Chanel, Gucci, Burberry, Louis Vuitton, Lacoste and Samsonite – with a range that covered bags, watches, jackets, shoes, shirts, shorts, belts, jeans, socks and underwear. Here you could bargain with the local vendors in broken English or punch bids and counter-bids into a pocket calculator. And here on a warm, autumn day in October 1997, the billionaire media mogul Rupert Murdoch was haggling over the price of some ties.

Murdoch was enthralled by the capitalist fervour of the enthusiastic stall holders in the market. He would remark at a dinner for some of Beijing's foreign correspondents later that evening that he was 'yet to meet a communist in China', adding half-jokingly, 'After all, isn't the Chinese Communist Party really just the world's largest Chamber of Commerce?'.

Squeezing his way through the thronging hordes, Murdoch went from stall to stall inspecting the goods and checking prices, until he came to a stand offering silk neckties. Beside him, Wendi Deng, just three days into her first assignment as Murdoch's interpreter on his trip to Shanghai and Beijing, offered some fashion advice as he selected various patterns and held them up against his shirt. When told the price of the ties was roughly 40 yuan, or four or five dollars each, an astounded Murdoch decided it was too good a bargain to pass up compared to the 100 dollars plus he normally paid for his neck attire back home. He selected seven ties and would have happily taken more had Wendi not suggested he might want to look at some other stalls to see what else was on offer.

Murdoch reached for his wallet. I explained to him that having selected his ties there were no fixed prices, so now he had to haggle with the vendor over how much he was prepared to pay.

'Right,' said Murdoch, eagerly squaring up to the young Chinese salesman, 'How much?'

'Two hundred forty,' came the offer, the vendor punching the numbers into a calculator and showing it to Murdoch so there could be no confusion.

'Two hundred sixty,' Murdoch shot back.

There was a stunned silence, before the collected group burst into laughter.

'No, no,' the vendor responded, slapping his thigh in mirth. 'You must offer lower, not higher.'

Murdoch good-naturedly conceded defeat with a wry smile. He handed over the 240 yuan — knowing full well he had overpaid, but convinced he had a bargain just the same.

He had probably felt the same sentiment four years earlier, when from the deck of his 48-metre luxury yacht *Morning Glory*, moored in the Mediterranean, he had negotiated the purchase of the fledgling STAR TV network from the 26-year-old Richard Li. Murdoch would end up paying close to US$1 billion to take full ownership of STAR (Satellite Television for the Asian Region). His critics would argue that he had paid far too much for an asset that was bleeding cash and had no viable business plan to rectify the haemorrhaging. Murdoch was convinced his instincts were right and that China would prove to be a financial bonanza. He loved nothing better than proving the naysayers wrong. Breaching the Great Wall of China would become a very personal obsession.

Rupert Murdoch's affair with China began in April 1985, when he made his first visit to the Middle Kingdom along with his then wife Anna, and the children, Elisabeth, Lachlan and James. His arrival was warmly anticipated by the Chinese authorities after the Australian Prime Minister, Bob Hawke, had widely extolled the virtues of Australia's most successful businessman to his Beijing counterparts during an official visit late the previous year. Hawke was keen on building a strong bilateral relationship with China and had established a very cordial dialogue with the country's reformist-minded leaders Hu Yaobang and Zhao Ziyang. He was actively encouraging Australian business to invest there.

In typical Murdoch fashion, even a family holiday had to make room for his business dealings and in between sightseeing visits to Shanghai, the terracotta warriors in Xian and the Great Wall, Murdoch found himself feted by his Chinese hosts at numerous official banquets. In the midst of the first stages of the economic modernisation and reform program that would turn the country on its head, the Chinese were in awe of Murdoch, who they knew had built a media empire from scratch and was now taking on the traditional market leaders in their own backyards in the US and Britain. Murdoch, in return, was astonished by the modernisation that was taking place and the rampant consumerism that it was producing. With a potential market of a billion or more customers, the tycoon believed this was a place he could do business.

Before his departure from Beijing he had already agreed on

his first investment in China. Oddly enough for Murdoch, it was not a media play, but a real estate development. On 2 May 1985, Murdoch announced a deal with the government-controlled China Central Television (CCTV) to invest US$40 million to build an international hotel and news media centre in Beijing. The centre, scheduled for completion just two years later, was to include a 300-room hotel and 100 apartments for journalists and business executives.

Under the deal, the Chinese would provide the land and handle the bureaucratic requirements while Murdoch's News Corporation would provide the money. Murdoch had indeed spotted an opening in the China market. Beijing was desperately short of quality accommodation and as the foreign press corps rapidly expanded there would be a captive market – the Chinese authorities could stipulate where the correspondents would be housed. What appealed to the budding media tycoon was the irony of being able to later gouge some of his bitterest corporate rivals for rent in a Murdoch-owned and operated hotel.

He instructed his Australian lieutenants, News Limited Chairman Ken Cowley and Corporate Development Director Malcolm Colless, to sort out the detail. One aspect of the deal proposed by the Chinese side was that the interest rate on their part of the US$40 million loan be fixed at 5 per cent, with the foreign partner (News Corporation) picking up the balance. With interest lending rates in Australia in 1987 close to reaching all-time highs of

16 per cent, Cowley and Colless were having second thoughts about the economics behind the proposed investment. They convinced Murdoch to quietly extricate himself from the arrangement, which he did by deftly passing it on to Sir Peter Abeles, his hapless co-owner of Ansett Airlines, the Australian aviation company of which he had acquired 50 per cent during his failed takeover attempt of the Melbourne-based Herald and Weekly Times media group in 1979. (Murdoch would go on to acquire the group, which had once been run by his father Sir Keith Murdoch, in 1987.)

Then, in late 1987, Murdoch snapped up Hong Kong's most profitable daily newspaper, the English-language *South China Morning Post*, for US$230 million – a bargain given the rivers of gold flowing from the paper's classified advertisements in a booming economy.

During the next few years, China took second place to Murdoch's own revolution – one that culminated in one of the most dramatic industrial disputes of the last century. Determined to break the vice-like grip of the powerful print unions on his British publishing operations, Murdoch secretly moved his newspaper business overnight to a fortress-like plant in Wapping, east London. The move sparked a bitter but ultimately doomed year-long strike by printers which revolutionised labour relations in the UK and forever changed the newspaper industry.

Murdoch followed one revolution with another. Next was the 5 February 1989 launch of his Sky Television satellite service, which would eventually form the basis of one of the most profit-able broadcast operations in the world when merged with rival British Satellite Broadcasting (BSB) to create BSkyB. But the cost of funding the early losses incurred by these operations, on top of new acquisitions in the US and Australia, meant News Corporation had amassed an inordinate amount of short-term debt to pay for it. Unable to meet its payments on time, the company was threatened with bankruptcy and the break-up of the empire. After Murdoch's well-documented escape from the clutches of his bankers during a period of torrid renegotiation of every single one of the company's loans during 1991, he went through a brief period of consolidation before another trip to Beijing in April 1993 reignited his passion for the China market and risk-taking on an extraordinary scale.

Murdoch's trip to China was ostensibly to make contact with his 'old friends' at CCTV to see if he could extend the interests of his Fox television network and to look for opportunities in its developing magazine sector. He believed that with an injection of some News Corp editorial nous, modern sales techniques and a decent colour press, the magazine market was there for the taking. Murdoch made an offer for a 50 per cent share in the state-owned *Better Life* magazine during his visit. It was politely turned down by the Beijing authorities.

However, during his time in Beijing Murdoch noted that he was able to receive a five-channel English-language television service at the hotel where he was staying, beamed by satellite from Hong

Kong. STAR TV was owned by Richard Li, the son of Hong Kong's wealthiest billionaire, Li Ka-shing, who was now making another fortune with investments across southern China. With a footprint across an area from the Philippines, China, South-East Asia, India and the Middle East, STAR TV had the potential to reach two-thirds of the world's population. Given his experience with BSkyB in the UK, which was now returning handsome profits, Murdoch was absolutely mesmerised by the possibilities inherent in a pan-regional satellite television service.

Richard Li was a precocious 23-year-old when he convinced his father to have the family company, Hutchison Whampoa, invest an initial US$62.5 million into building Asia's first satellite television network. The younger Li had been at schools in the US since the age of thirteen before attending, but not graduating from, Stanford University. His billionaire father kept him on a strict budget and Richard made extra money by working as a caddie at a golf course and manning a cash register at McDonald's. After graduation in 1987, he worked as fund manager at a Canadian investment bank and then in 1990 was summoned home to take charge of Hutchison's satellite unit.

Li soon came to realise that the satellite Hutchison was using for its telecommunications services was also capable of beaming television signals via its transponders. He was convinced that the collapse of the former Soviet Union was a sure sign that communism would soon fail everywhere and national borders would dissolve, thereby allowing him to circumvent the government monopolies that controlled TV throughout Asia by beaming programs directly to viewers.

The STAR TV service launched in 1991 with just five channels. Four of them were broadcast in English: MTV Asia, BBC World Service News, a sports channel and an entertainment channel that depended on syndicated programs from the US, including Oprah Winfrey's talk show, reruns of American series such as *Dynasty* and *Dr. Kildare*, and old movies. The fifth channel featured a hodge-podge of Chinese-language entertainment.

Li's plans envisaged millions of Asians rushing out to sign up to the new satellite service. What he didn't envisage was the innate entrepreneurship of Chinese consumers. Rather than subscribe to the new service, they pirated the signal and redistributed it for their own benefit. The STAR TV signal was unencrypted and simply rained down from the sky for free. Official satellite dishes were expensive until the Chinese introduced cheap copies. Smart businessmen soon realised it was far cheaper to distribute the channels by cable and that the service could be captured at very little cost and redistributed for a profit. Very soon, tens of thousands of entrepreneurs across China were installing cheap satellite dishes and stringing rolls of copper wire down the streets and through the trees to their neighbours' homes, charging up to two dollars a month for the service.

Li changed tack with his business plan and decided that his

best option was to actively encourage the pirating and redistribution of the signal, on the basis that STAR TV would make its money purely by assembling the largest possible audience and selling advertising to it.

By April 1993 Richard Li was widely touting the success of the company, claiming some 45 million viewers in 11 million homes, and US$300 million in advertising commitments from 360 advertisers. But there was, in fact, no means of measuring the audience at all. The figures were at best brave assumptions, while the advertising commitments remained just that – commitments, not cold hard cash. Hutchison Whampoa's financial reports at the time indicated the company had injected US$125 million over the first two years and was still losing in the order of US$90 million a year.

Richard Li started to come under immense pressure from both his father and the Hutchison Whampoa senior executives to get out of STAR TV, not just because of the immense losses it was incurring, but also the political grief it was causing in Beijing.

Only some years later, in 1997, did I learn from my Chinese foreign ministry contacts that the Beijing leadership, which had given tacit agreement to the launch of the satellite service, felt they had been betrayed by Richard Li. The young Li, it seems, had indicated in his discussions with the authorities that the satellite footprint would cover just the southern coastal areas of China – particularly Guangdong province, which because of its close proximity to Hong Kong was already open to cultural influences from the outside world. When STAR TV commenced broadcasting, the national security services were outraged to learn that the signal covered the entire country, and that anyone with the money to purchase a cheap receiver dish could capture and redistribute the 'spiritually polluting' content.

Li Ka-shing, however, was not only one of the single biggest foreign investors in China, he was also a confidant of the Paramount Leader, Deng Xiaoping, and the new President, Jiang Zemin. The Chinese bureaucrats were unwilling to take any overt action which might lead to a 'loss of face' for a man widely seen to be one of the most generous and loyal overseas Chinese patriots. It was made known to him that certain elements of the ruling elite were extremely unhappy with STAR TV and that it would be in his company's interests to divest its interest in the broadcaster.

Richard Li was a reluctant seller, but in May 1993 he agreed to put STAR TV on the market. There were in reality just two interested parties: Pearson PLC, owner of the *Financial Times* and Penguin books among other media interests, and Rupert Murdoch's News Corporation. Pearson was widely thought to have had the inside running. The company had previously enjoyed a long relationship with Li Ka-shing in the 1980s when he had held a stake in Pearson, although he later sold it to Murdoch in 1987, who in turn had to dispose of it during his early '90s debt crisis. Both companies saw STAR TV as a perfect fit for their Asian expansion strategies although neither, it seemed, questioned why Li Ka-shing, one of Asia's shrewdest and most successful tycoons – a man with very deep pockets who in the past had shown his preparedness to wear massive financial losses over many years to see projects through – was so keen to bail out of it.

Pearson executives would later reveal that while they had been offered the same deal as Murdoch, to purchase 64 per cent of STAR TV, the alarm bells began to ring for them when the elder Li declined to provide a guarantee that he would stay on and assist the venture in gaining access to the China market. Pearson, with little experience in the ways of doing business in Asia, hesitated at the thought of going it alone.

Murdoch has no such qualms. He was vacationing with the family in the Mediterranean aboard the *Morning Glory* – a beautiful azure-hulled luxury ketch he had purchased at Anna's suggestion two years earlier. She thought it might allow Murdoch the opportunity to relax and unwind. When Murdoch heard that Pearson was hesitating in its deliberations, he interrupted the family holiday to invite Richard Li and his advisers for a 'chat' on the boat. A deal to purchase 64 per cent of STAR TV for US$525 million was negotiated in a matter of hours. Murdoch didn't bother to inform his own board until later that the deal had been done.

Richard Li had also not bothered to inform the Chinese authorities of his decision to sell, or the identity of STAR TV's new owner, until the deal was a fait accompli. There was already great suspicion about satellite television amongst the ranks of the leadership –

especially those who had watched the events of the Tiananmen Square uprising unfold live in their living rooms via CNN just a few years earlier. The Politburo – the centre of power in the Chinese Communist Party – believed at the very least that Li Ka-shing was a trusted ally and compatriot who had no political designs on China. He could be relied upon to do the right thing by China and pull the plug on STAR TV if necessity demanded. But now it was not just in the hands of a foreigner, but in the hands of Rupert Murdoch. While Murdoch professed to be a friend of China, the Chinese were well aware of his proclivity to involve himself in a nation's politics if it were to the advantage of his business interests. That Richard Li had not sought the imprimatur of Beijing prior to closing the transaction was yet another blot on his record. Richard was fast running out of *guanxi* ('powerful connections') in Beijing.

If Murdoch thought he could rely on the elder Li to help ease the way in Beijing, it soon proved otherwise. When the media tycoon approached Li Ka-shing, he received some friendly advice and little else. Li was content to have washed his hands of the troublesome broadcaster. Technically, STAR TV was out of reach of the Chinese government, based as it was in Hong Kong, then still a British colony, and legally Murdoch needed no approval from any government to broadcast his television channels from space.

Murdoch had his bargain, even if he had overpaid. It was the Asian counterpart to his Fox network in the US and BSkyB in Britain and gave him an unrivalled reach around the globe. In the media,

Murdoch's daring in snapping up STAR TV from under the noses of Pearson was hailed as a masterstroke. He had purchased the potential to reach nearly three billion people – almost two-thirds of the world's population. Murdoch was well on the way to building the first truly global television empire.

If there were suspicions and restrictions from Asian governments concerned about the impact of Western programming on Asian values, Murdoch remained supremely confident of his ability to deal with any hostility. As he had so many times before, in so many countries, Murdoch believed that if he could just sit down and talk with the political leader in question, an accommodation could be reached that was to the mutual benefit of all concerned.

In Beijing, the Chinese government made no comment. The Politburo members sat on their hands, despite the urgings of more conservative elements. The Chinese authorities were uncertain how to react and were waiting for Murdoch to show his hand – friend or foe, avowed libertarian or pragmatic businessman. When he did, just five weeks after the announcement of his acquisition of STAR TV, the media mogul left them in no doubt as to where he stood.

As a result, the Chinese responded in kind, leaving Murdoch clearly aware of where *they* felt he stood – and that was outside the Great Wall of China.

2

Whoops

London's Banqueting House is the only remaining complete building of Whitehall Palace, the British sovereign's principal residence from 1530 until 1698, when it was destroyed by fire. Designed in the Palladian style, its centrepiece is a great cubic hall featuring striking Ionic columns, enormous corniced windows and a ceiling painted by Rubens. It was originally built for grand occasions of state, plays and elaborate pageants.

It was an apt setting for a speech by the man widely seen as heading up the world's fastest-growing media empire. Here, on 1 September 1993, the now flourishing satellite television company BSkyB had invited hundreds of the city's advertising executives and media buyers to a lavish function to celebrate the launch of its new multi-channel offering. The highlight of the evening was a speech by BSkyB Chairman Rupert Murdoch on the virtues of a new technology that would forever change the media paradigm.

This was a defining moment for Murdoch. Just three years earlier his critics had written him off. News Corp had faced a massive liquidity crisis in 1990 – a combination of the costs incurred by his start-up British satellite television venture, the recession, huge drops in advertising revenues worldwide and an over-reliance on short-term debt at a time of rising interest rates. News Corp had US$7.6 billion in debt owed to 146 different institutions and all of it needed to be rolled over in a hurry. Murdoch, as he later admitted, 'had taken [his] eye off the ball' and was in danger of losing his empire.

But once again Murdoch's charm and persuasion had come to the fore. With a good deal of support from Citibank in restructuring News Corp's debt, some strategic asset sales and a rebounding economy, he had not only survived his 'near-death experience', but in 1993 he was back on the acquisition trail. In July, he had bought 63.6 per cent of STAR TV. He had also agreed to acquire one of the United States' first internet providers, Delphi Internet Service, a Massachusetts-based computer network with some 50 000 customers. Murdoch was additionally about to regain ownership of the influential *New York Post*, which he'd been forced to sell in 1988 to further his television interests in the US.

More importantly, the previously loss-making satellite service BSkyB was now the toast of London and the envy of the entire media industry. In 1990 the satellite broadcaster's losses were in excess of US$25 million a week. The turning point had come in

1992 when, with BBC backing, BSkyB offered close to US$600 million for the exclusive rights to broadcast the UK Premier League's live football matches. As a result, BSkyB was able to offer a new encrypted subscription service which attracted more than a million additional viewers within months of going on offer.

By mid-1992 BSkyB was showing its first operating profits, of around US$200 000 per week. As Murdoch climbed the stairs to the podium at Banqueting House he knew that in that current fiscal year alone the broadcaster was headed for an operating profit of some US$350 million. It was indeed a remarkable turnaround. And with the purchase of the stake in STAR TV, Murdoch was planning to emulate his success in the largest television market of all – China.

The speech was very much about News Corp being at the forefront of the communications revolution that was taking place. In 1993, even though the internet was still in its infancy, the talk was very much of 'information superhighways' and 'electronic data networks' moving information seamlessly around the planet. And indeed, Murdoch and News Corp had leap-frogged the competition, leading the way in satellite television, compression technology, encryption systems and online video services. Murdoch was justifiably buoyant as he delivered his speech, reeling off the extraordinary achievements made possible by the new communications technology.

A key point of the speech was that in his book *1984*, George

Orwell had got it wrong – mass communications technology was not in fact a totalitarian means of subordinating the individual, but a liberator.

'Advances in the technology of telecommunications have proved an unambiguous threat to totalitarian regimes everywhere,' Murdoch said. 'Fax machines enable dissidents to bypass state-controlled print media. Direct-dial telephony makes it difficult for a state to control interpersonal voice communications. And satellite broadcasting makes it possible for information-hungry residents of many closed societies to bypass state-controlled television channels.'

We later learnt that when the first reports of Murdoch's speech reached the Chinese leadership compound at Zhongnanhai, eight thousand kilometres away in Beijing, Premier Li Peng was incandescent with rage. Premier Li was one of the most unpopular politicians in China, mainly for his lack of charisma, his image as a hardliner and his role in suppressing the Tiananmen Square protests. Dubbed 'the Butcher of Beijing' for his instrumental part in the 1989 crackdown, including the declaration of martial law and the final order for the troops to move in and disperse the student protesters from the square, Li had good reason to think that Murdoch's comments were very much directed at the Beijing leadership.

China's student-led democracy movement in 1989 was in fact largely orchestrated by fax machine. The protesters used the fax machines to circumvent the normal telephone lines, which were being closely monitored by the Chinese security forces, to coordinate the activities of the democracy movement, organising demonstrations and meeting points and culminating in over one million people rallying in Beijing's Tiananmen Square to call for the Chinese government to embrace political reforms. Overseas supporters of the protest movement also used fax machines to send news of how the Western media were reporting events, which greatly buoyed the spirits and enthusiasm of the student leaders, and encouraged them to continue with their struggle.

So concerned was the Chinese leadership with the perceived role of the ubiquitous fax machine that on 4 June 1989, the day that government troops entered Tiananmen Square to end the democracy movement, it attempted to deploy monitors at every fax machine in China to intercept foreign reports about the events – albeit without much success.

But it was the live television news coverage of the lead-up, the protests, the unveiling of the 10-metre high Goddess of Democracy, and the eventual bloody crackdown being beamed not just by satellite to the outside world but back again via CNN into the leadership and official compounds of China, that really rattled Beijing's ruling elite.

The previous month, the authorities had allowed the news correspondents with their satellite dishes and up-linking equipment into the country in order to cover the historic visit to Beijing by Soviet Union President Mikhail Gorbachev for the first Sino-Soviet summit since 1959. The rapidly escalating democracy movement soon overshadowed the Gorbachev meeting and the Chinese leadership found itself confounded by the international coverage delivered to their homes and offices of the mounting protests rather than the new détente between Moscow and Beijing. The students themselves had grown increasingly bold in both their protests and their demands, buoyed by the presence of so many international correspondents and film crews. The Chinese leadership appeared paralysed, unable to come to terms with the unfolding drama on their doorstep.

The turning point, however, was the televised image of student leader Wang Dan seated on a sofa, weak from hunger, summoning the strength and sheer nerve to publicly scold a poker-faced Premier Li Peng, who had mistakenly attempted to lecture the students on appropriate behaviour. The scene was broadcast not just in China but to the world, and it was that event, the public humiliation and loss of face, that hardened Li Peng's resolve to crush the democracy movement regardless of cost.

The resulting crackdown on 4 June left the world with some of the most memorable and shattering images of modern times – the tanks from the People's Liberation Army rolling into Tiananmen Square, the lone protester with his shopping bag attempting to stem their advance, bicycle trolleys rushing the dead and wounded from the carnage that was occurring in the streets leading to the square, and the toppling of the Goddess of Democracy.

Tiananmen Square was an international public relations disaster for China that set back its economic reforms by years and tarnished its image in the eyes of the West for a decade after. And while Premier Li may have in fact been simply carrying out the orders of Party elders, including Paramount Leader Deng Xiaoping, it was he who would wear the opprobrium of the West's condemnation.

And less than four years later, Rupert Murdoch, the new owner of a satellite network capable of beaming its signal across the entire Chinese nation, seemingly rubbed the noses of the Chinese leadership in the bloody debacle of 1989. Li Peng took the comments not just as a personal insult but as a premeditated and calculated threat by Murdoch to Chinese sovereignty.

Within a month of the Banqueting House speech, Premier Li had personally signed a decree banning the distribution, installation and use of satellite reception dishes anywhere in China. The Murdoch dream in China was permanently on hold.

Years later, riding in the back of a limousine from Beijing Airport into the city for yet another round of official meetings, I asked Murdoch just how the speech – or, in any case, that particularly infamous line about the 'unambiguous threat to totalitarian regimes' – came about. He claimed that Irwin Stelzer, the American economist, *Sunday Times* columnist and Murdoch confidant, had written it for him.

'I read through it in the afternoon before the speech and just didn't pick it up – not in the context of China,' he said. 'I was really thinking in terms of all that happened in the Soviet Union, the

Berlin Wall coming down. It didn't dawn on me that it would be portrayed as it was.'

The CEO of STAR TV, Gary Davey, and I would often joke afterwards that, word for word, Murdoch's remarks were probably the costliest ever uttered by an individual.

Needless to say, Murdoch's explanation that he had been referring to the old Soviet bloc and not his friends, the Chinese, found little sway amongst the Beijing leadership. After all, by 1993 totalitarian regimes were in short supply – East Germany had all but disappeared and the old Soviet Union and its puppet states were in disarray. It didn't leave a whole lot of other prime suspects. In my discussions and attempts at extricating Murdoch from the hole he had dug, the Chinese would also point out that the speech made direct references to the fax machine and the ability of satellite technology to bypass 'state-controlled television channels', leaving them in no doubt to which country he was referring.

For Premier Li Peng and the Politburo elite, it was akin to a declaration of war.

Only ten years later, in discussions with contacts at China's Ministry of Foreign Affairs, did I learn just how seriously the Chinese had taken Murdoch's comments.

Premier Li, it transpired, ensured that Murdoch's apparent threat was raised at a meeting of the entire Chinese Politburo – the body which comprises the highest-ranked decision makers of the Chinese Communist Party. Chaired by the Party General Secretary,

Jiang Zemin, the Politburo agreed that so serious were the imputations contained in the media tycoon's speech that a team headed by the nation's Security Chief, Luo Gan, together with the powerful head of the Propaganda Department, Ding Guangen, would be responsible for drawing up a strategy to deal with Murdoch and protect the nation from the 'unambiguous threat' posed by the new communication technologies.

Luo Gan was a protégé of Li Peng and was widely thought to have given the orders to the armed police of the Public Security Bureau during the crackdown on the Tiananmen Square protesters. He held the influential position of Secretary to the State Council but, more ominously, he also headed the Political and Legislative Affairs Committee, which made him responsible for 'law and order' throughout the country, including its foreign and counter-intelligence work.

Comrade Luo was also hailed as having instituted China's 'strike hard' campaign, which targeted criminal activity across the nation and resulted in a record number of prosecutions, trials and hasty executions.

Comrade Ding was an engineer by training and spent thirty years of his career in the Ministry of Railways, rising through the ranks to become Minister in the early 1980s. However, it was his exceptional bridge-playing skills that brought him to the attention of China's other great cards enthusiast, Deng Xiaoping. Ding became the Paramount Leader's favoured bridge partner in a card game widely played by the ruling elite. International bridge players visiting Beijing for a tournament would sometimes find themselves invited to a private audience and a round of cards with Deng and his loyal offsider. They were regarded as formidable opponents.

With the aid of Deng's patronage, Ding had rapidly advanced through the ranks of the Chinese leadership hierarchy. By 1993 he was a full member of the Politburo and a year earlier had been named the new head of the Propaganda Department.

The Propaganda Department is an internal division of the Communist Party of China and, while not formally a part of government, it is the de facto highest office enforcing censorship and control over every facet of the media in China and is responsible for projecting and protecting the nation's image at home and abroad.

Ding, in particular, would become Murdoch's nemesis over the next decade. Every move Murdoch made in China would be matched or blocked by a counter-move from Ding and his minions. The English-speaking Propaganda Chief – ironically a great fan of Hollywood movie classics – would over the years build up an extraordinary dossier on Murdoch and every aspect of News Corporation's operations around the world. It was Ding who would control the media giant's advance in China.

The Chinese were all too aware of the role an unchecked media and newly found freedom of expression had had in bringing about the collapse of the former Soviet Union. They were convinced Murdoch would do everything possible to gain unfettered access to the China market. Indeed, over the next four years, I would be constantly asked by government officials in hushed tones if it were true that Murdoch had a war chest of US$1 billion at his disposal to bludgeon his way into the living rooms of China's television audience.

Murdoch's defining moment in London would come back to haunt him in China. The Chinese leadership had arrayed its very considerable forces to defend itself against any News Corp incursion into its territory. Beijing was determined that it would monitor his every step in their backyard, and that any move by the world's most influential 'capitalist roader' would be at a place, a pace and a timing determined by them.

Rupert Murdoch, of course, had other ideas.

3

Deng Rong! The King is Dead

Beijing in the summer is often referred to by the locals as 'the stove'. Stifling, oppressive; the temperatures remain consistently in the high thirties and the humidity touches 95 per cent. August of 1994 was no different. Women in their summer dresses walked under protective pastel parasols fending off the harsh sun. Construction workers and shopkeepers rolled up their T-shirts to just below nipple level, displaying their modest torsos in any attempt to find relief from the sweltering, unrelenting heat.

Only Rupert Murdoch remained out in the cold in Beijing. The Chinese leadership was intent on punishing him for the disastrous Whitehall Palace speech of the previous September and was rejecting every overture for reconciliation.

Murdoch knew that he had made a serious mistake. He had already divested himself of his most profitable newspaper, the *South China Morning Post*, rather than risk it causing offence to the

26

Chinese government in the lead-up to the 1997 handover of Hong Kong. Murdoch had consulted the *Post*'s new owner, billionaire Malaysian-Chinese businessman Robert Kwok, who was known to have impeccable credentials with China's political elite. Kwok's advice was that the world's most powerful media tycoon should get himself up to Beijing as often as possible and knock on doors in order to convince the powers-that-be that he was a friend, not an enemy, of China.

The problem for Murdoch was that not only were the Chinese not listening – at least no one that really mattered – but they were refusing to open the doors to his persistent knocking.

Ding Guangen had issued strict instructions through the State Council Information Office (SCIO) that every request for a meeting from Murdoch or his representatives would be reported to him at the Propaganda Department. In what was a very pointed and calculated snub, it was decreed that the world's most successful media baron would meet no official of a rank above vice minister. This at a time when Time Warner's Gerald 'Jerry' Levin and Viacom's Sumner Redstone were both getting more senior access.

Requests for meetings with the head of CCTV, Yang Weiguang, were fobbed off on more junior officials. The SCIO Minister, Zeng Jianhui, had issued instructions that when such meetings did take place, the Chinese present were to be polite and courteous but no more. In no event should approval be given for any joint venture or undertakings of any kind. Furthermore, he appointed his offsider,

Li Bing, to maintain a specific watch on News Corporation's activities in China.

To get himself closer to the source of his problem, Murdoch took the surprising step of moving house to Hong Kong in late 1993, renting a mansion high on the Peak, the colony's most prestigious address. Anna moved from the US West Coast and completely redecorated the new home. Unfortunately the couple's arrival coincided with Hong Kong's notorious winter. The Peak was largely covered in cloud the whole time – the otherwise spectacular views were shrouded in mist and smog. According to Rupert, Anna was not impressed. The Murdochs moved back to Los Angeles after just six weeks.

Meantime, Murdoch was looking for a circuit breaker. In April 1994 he thought he had found one. In consultation with Gary Davey, who he had brought over from the number two job at the now successful BSkyB to become the new CEO of STAR TV, Murdoch decided to drop the BBC from the northern signal of the STAR TV satellite service. Davey claimed that given the limited transponder space available on the satellite, a Chinese-language movie channel was a far better commercial proposition than having News Corporation pay for the carriage of an English-language news service produced by the BBC. Never a great fan of the BBC – or any public broadcaster for that matter – Murdoch had also heard from a variety of sources that the Chinese hierarchy had been deeply offended by a BBC documentary on Chairman Mao Zedong, which touched in part on the leader's rather unusual sexual predilections. The spin was to be that it was a 'purely commercial decision' – the BBC had to go to make way for a new movie channel – although Murdoch would later tell biographer William Shawcross that the Chinese leaders 'hated the BBC'. He said, 'They say it's a cowardly way, but we said in order to get in there and get accepted we'll cut the BBC out.'

Murdoch was very roundly condemned by commentators around the world and the Governor of Hong Kong, Chris Patten, described it as 'the most seedy of betrayals'.

In fact, it wasn't just the BBC. Murdoch told me later that it 'didn't matter what news service you carried, you were always going to agitate someone. If not the Chinese, the Malaysians or Thais. It's just not worth the trouble'.

If the move was welcomed in Beijing, it was never acknowledged, at least not at the time. The ban on satellite dishes remained firmly in place. Murdoch was still *persona non grata*.

Undeterred, the media tycoon was about to embark on a new tack.

Eric Walsh, a former political correspondent for the News Limited newspapers in Canberra before becoming press secretary to Labor Prime Minister Gough Whitlam soon after his election in 1972, had since established himself as a well-connected Canberra lobbyist. Walsh's connections were very much in the back room of the Australian Labor Party and he was owed a good many favours by any number of public service mandarins whose careers he had aided while a close confidant of the former Prime Minister. Walsh himself had little international experience, although as a member of the media he had accompanied Whitlam on his groundbreaking visit to Beijing in 1973, making Australia one of the first Western nations to restore normal relations with the Communist giant.

Walsh had remained in contact with Murdoch and by late 1993 had convinced his old boss that a close acquaintance, and business partner of EJ Walsh and Associates, might just have the necessary *guanxi* (connections) in China to put STAR TV back on track.

And there she was, in August 1994, standing on the footpath outside Robert Kwok's new China World Hotel complex dressed in white hotpants and a bright yellow T-shirt. Linda Lau was a vivacious, chatty forty-something Australian-Chinese who hadn't set foot in China for thirty years until she got the gig with Murdoch. But she carried a business card announcing her as News Corporation's 'Director, China'.

I had only recently arrived in Beijing to begin negotiations with the *People's Daily* newspaper on a possible joint venture. Murdoch had suggested I meet with Lau and discuss it with her. Sitting down over a coffee, I outlined the discussions with *People's Daily*, to which she was fairly dismissive.

'Rupert needs to go to the top,' she said. 'If Deng gives his approval, everything will be okay.'

By 'Deng' she meant Comrade Deng Xiaoping – China's

patriarch, under whose tutelage the nation developed one of the fastest-growing economies in the world while maintaining absolute Communist Party control, and on whom the world leaders slavishly doted until he ordered the bloody slaughter that was Tiananmen Square.

Lau went on to drop the names of various Deng family siblings whom she was apparently in contact with – daughters Deng Lin, Deng Nan and Deng Rong, and sons Deng Pufang and Deng Zhifang. She was convinced that by courting the Deng children Murdoch's influence would grow with the 'old man', and a nod from him would bring about certain rehabilitation and open skies for the STAR TV platform. Lau had Rupert's ear and he was listening.

Lau had befriended Deng Rong, the youngest of the Paramount Leader's children. Rong, known more commonly by her nickname 'Maomao', had long been the most visible of the Deng siblings, often acting as her father's personal secretary and translator during meetings with foreign dignitaries in his later life. She had penned a biography, *My Father: Deng Xiaoping*, which had become a bestseller in China. Lau had earlier persuaded Murdoch it would be in his interests to pay an advance to secure the English-language rights to the book.

The News Corp subsidiary HarperCollins promptly secured the rights to the book. When I asked Murdoch how much we had paid for the advance he was unusually vague about the amount, which led me to believe it was far more than he was prepared to admit to – probably less than the US$1 million that appeared in the media reports, but perhaps not much less.

When news of the deal surfaced, Murdoch critics immediately branded it as a blatant attempt to buy favour in China. But it was also true that there was a great deal of interest in the West about the Paramount Leader Deng Xiaoping, who had inspired an economic revolution of epic proportions. Murdoch was undoubtedly impressed by the changes he had seen wrought in China under Deng's stewardship and may well have been trusting his publisher's instinct that the book would find a market outside China. Unfortunately, someone at HarperCollins might have done well to have read the English translation before agreeing to the advance.

When it appeared, the book was clearly at best a very broad-stroke portrait of a father by a loving daughter. *The New York Times* perhaps predictably labelled it a 'turgid, barely literate propaganda piece'. Other reviews declared it 'decidedly dull'.

Murdoch, however, did his very best to promote it. In February 1995 he turned up at the party to launch the book at New York's exclusive Waldorf Astoria, before hosting a private dinner party for some fifty guests at the elegant Le Cirque on the Upper East Side. The guests included a who's who of Washington and New York. Murdoch followed up on the west coast with a private lunch for Maomao at his ranch in Carmel, California.

Just three months later it was Deng Pufang's turn to be on the receiving end of the full Murdoch royal treatment. The eldest son of the China Patriarch, Deng Pufang had experienced firsthand the terror of the Cultural Revolution when he 'fell' from a four-storey building while being harassed by the fanatical Red Guards. The fall broke his spine and paralysed him from the waist down. But with the restoration of his father to power in 1978, the paraplegic Pufang used his connections to create the Chinese Federation for the Disabled.

Deng Pufang had been invited to Australia to promote the Asia and Pacific Decade of Disabled Persons 1993–2002. He planned to bring with him a thirty-strong disabled performing arts troupe, made up of blind, deaf and physically disabled artists, with the intention of staging performances in Canberra and Sydney to raise funds for the United Nations' disabled persons programs.

Advance ticket sales to the performances were so poor that the organisers became concerned that they would have to cancel the event. Through Linda Lau's intervention, Murdoch agreed that News Corporation – with some financial contributions from Australian Telecom (now Telstra) and Cadbury Schweppes – would underwrite the entire tour. News Corp employees were also made aware that it would be in their best interests to take advantage of free tickets on hand in order that the auditorium had some semblance of being filled.

In fact, Deng Pufang, on his first trip to Australia, was very much impressed by the facilities and resources made available to the disabled in the country and in later speeches would often hold it up as a model for China to emulate.

Murdoch was unable to travel to Australia to meet personally with Deng Pufang, but Lau persuaded him that the performing troupe might need a chance to recover from the rigours of their tour. Keen to make the maximum impression, he agreed to fly the entire troupe by private plane to Hayman Island in Queensland's Whitsunday Island group for a week of rest and recuperation – all expenses paid. Hayman Island in 1995 was one of the most luxurious and expensive luxury resorts in the world. Fortunately it was then owned by the Ansett Airlines group – which, in turn, was owned by Murdoch.

For a full week the thirty-strong disabled performing troupe enjoyed the exclusive attention of the Hayman Island staff, swimming, dining, game fishing and sailing, all at Murdoch's, or more correctly News Corp's, expense. At the end of it, Linda Lau suggested that they might take the private plane and continue the tour on to New Zealand. Even Murdoch baulked at that one. Deng Pufang, however, was profoundly impressed by the hospitality and Murdoch made a long-time friend.

Certainly, Murdoch felt sufficiently buoyed following his excursions with the Deng siblings that just two months later he concluded a deal with Hutchison Whampoa to buy the 36.4 per cent of STAR TV he did not already own, paying out an additional US$300 million. Coupled with the operating losses he was incurring every month, News Corp's exposure in China now topped the US$1 billion mark. And even though the satellite dish ban remained in place and the advertisers were staying away in droves, Murdoch was now confident things were about to change for the better.

Back on the ground in Beijing, neither STAR TV's Gary Davey nor myself, as Director of Business Development (Asia) for News Corp and in the midst of joint venture negotiations with the *People's Daily* newspaper, noticed any alteration in the frosty, formal reception we were receiving from our counterparts at CCTV and the Ministry for Radio, Film and Television. Truth be told, we were going backwards.

In fact, the ink was barely dry on Deng Rong's book publishing contract when the Great Patriarch of China made his last public appearance – a Chinese New Year visit to a bridge opening in Shanghai in February 1994. By mid-year the reports were that he had slipped into a coma, possibly as a result of pancreatic cancer and successive strokes. While mystery surrounded the true state of his health it was apparent that China was already entering the post-Deng era and that the power of the Deng princelings to influence government policy was very much on the wane.

While Deng had stepped down from all official positions in 1989, in a relatively smooth transition of power, his successor, Jiang Zemin, clearly did not hold the 'emperor' status enjoyed by the Paramount Leader. Jiang was struggling to consolidate his position and install his own people in key positions of power and influence.

Although he held the office of President and headed both the Communist Party and the army, questions were being raised about his staying power. Many Western observers saw him as little more than a transitional figure.

Jiang was intent on showing the Chinese people, and the world, that he was indeed now the boss and in charge. He embarked on a 'de-Dengification' of China, promoting his own ideology of 'spiritual civilisation' for the nation – a direct attack on the moneymaking culture that Deng created with the economic reforms he kicked off in 1978. In 1994, Jiang allowed political rivals to engineer the downfall of a close Deng family associate, Zhou Guanwu.

Next to fall was Mr Zhou's son, who ran a Hong Kong property development company; he was arrested for unspecified 'economic crimes'. The Vice Chairman and Chief Executive of the company was none other than Deng's younger son, Zhifang. Meanwhile reports surfaced in Beijing that Deng Pufang himself was being investigated for corruption – charges he vehemently denied.

Jiang Zemin was sending a very clear message to the Deng princelings: they were no longer a protected species. The emperor, if not dead, was slowly being buried.

Rupert Murdoch hadn't heard the message. At the very time Jiang Zemin was manoeuvring to exert his authority on the Chinese leadership, the world's most powerful media magnate was paying homage to Comrade Deng and his siblings as if they still ran the country. The level of irritation with Murdoch within the walls of the Chinese leadership compound at Zhongnanhai was palpable, I was later told.

If Beijing summers are stifling, the winters offer no comfort either. When Murdoch visited the capital in December 1995, it was clear the assiduous courting of the Deng family had come to naught. Meetings were once again relegated to vice ministers and lesser officials. The chill was worse than the cold, dry Arctic blast that blew in across the Gobi Desert and turned the city's ponds to ice.

4

Strange Bedfellows

It was the most unlikely of marriages. On the one side, the staid, conservative Communist Party newspaper of record and socialist rhetoric, *People's Daily*; on the other, Rupert Murdoch's News Corporation, the world's leading publisher of the sensationalist, muckraking, gossipy tabloid. That the courtship should begin in the VIP meeting room of the *People's Daily* Beijing compound beneath the baleful stare of a towering marble bust of China's Great Helmsman, Mao Zedong, added to the surreal nature of the event.

The cultural challenges posed by the potential partnership were made even more obvious when the two sides stopped for lunch on the first day of discussions and a meal was served – cold hamburgers and fries. Concerned that their foreign guests' palates would not be able to handle the local cuisine, they had sent out to the newly opened McDonald's restaurant in order to not offend us. Eating a cold McDonald's Big Mac was one thing; doing it with a pair of chopsticks was quite another.

By mid-1994 Murdoch was fully aware that the Chinese authorities had every intention of enforcing the total ban on satellite receiving dishes they had imposed following his ill-advised Whitehall Palace speech to advertisers the previous September. Initially, the authorities had been slow to move on confiscating the estimated 500 000 dishes that were scattered throughout the nation's rapidly developing urban centres. But in the first quarter of 1994 it was clear the Public Security Bureau had set about its task in earnest. The crackdown followed a speech early in the new year by Premier Li Peng at a conference on state security, in which – in remarks most commentators concluded were directed at Murdoch – he said: 'Hostile forces outside our country have never stopped endangering the safety of our country . . . [using] all means to infiltrate, split and damage us.'

STAR TV's five satellite channels could potentially be seen in thirty-eight nations in Asia and the Middle East, reaching, by STAR's estimates, 45 million households from Tokyo to Tel Aviv, Mongolia to Malaysia, and all of China and India. Murdoch's reputation for playing politics in the West was already resulting in a wave of criticism from Asian leaders, particularly Prime Minister Mahathir Mohamad of Malaysia, concerned about the impact of STAR TV's programming on the region's social and moral values. Mahathir had even suggested the media tycoon wanted 'to control the news that we are going to receive in Asia, otherwise why would Mr Murdoch, a naturalised American citizen from Australia, have paid such a fantastic price for a network that has never shown any profit?'

Murdoch continued to insist that he had no intention of interfering in the political affairs of the nations that received STAR TV and that he intended to make STAR a service that 'Asian families can enjoy in their homes' and one that Asian governments will consider both 'friendly and useful'.

The Chinese authorities remained unconvinced and while the satellite ban was in place in China, Murdoch was missing the key to the most potentially lucrative part of his Asian empire. News Corporation, by most accounts, had overpaid for STAR TV, but did so because Murdoch was convinced he had at least a two-year head start over his rivals, who would have to wait until new satellites were launched before they could begin broadcasting.

But by early 1994 there were already indications that Dow Jones & Company, the owner of *The Wall Street Journal*, was planning to start Asia's first satellite business news channel (later CNBC Asia). Its partners were said to include Tele-Communications Inc., the largest cable television company in the United States. There were also reports that a satellite network in competition with STAR TV would be launched by a powerful new consortium formed by the Turner Broadcasting System, the parent of CNN; Time Warner, parent of the year-old Home Box Office Asia; Capital Cities/ABC, majority owner of the ESPN sports channel; and TVB, the dominant television network in Hong Kong.

TVB's involvement in a rival consortium worried Murdoch, since it controlled the world's largest library of Cantonese-language television programs, which were seen as the key to television markets in Hong Kong and Taiwan and, importantly, to a vast potential audience in southern China where Cantonese was the dominant dialect. A month prior to his purchase of STAR TV, Murdoch had made an offer to buy 22.2 per cent of TVB, but was rebuffed by the Hong Kong regulatory authorities amid hints of displeasure from officials in Beijing.

Murdoch was increasingly agitated at the thought that his rivals were eating into his head start while he continued to bicker with Beijing. In fact, in private conversation he often seemed genuinely surprised that the Chinese leadership had taken so much offence over what he regarded as a 'few throwaway lines' in a speech. He was convinced that rather than him personally, Beijing's real anger was directed against the BBC World television service. Although he had already made the decision to drop the BBC from the STAR TV China signal, there had been no signs of the move having been welcomed by Beijing.

So Murdoch was buoyed when at about the same time he received word that there had been an unsolicited approach from a Chinese-American businessman, via the *New York Post*, about a proposal from *People's Daily* for a joint venture with News Corp to publish a

Chinese-language business magazine. Murdoch was hopeful that it was an indication 'all was forgiven' in Beijing, and that the authorities were sending a subtle message that he was off the blacklist. He also thought that a *BusinessWeek*-style magazine tapping into China's booming economy could well be a profitable venture. He passed the proposal on to his Australian lieutenant, Ken Cowley, to follow up. Cowley dispatched a delegation to Beijing headed by his Corporate Development Director, Malcolm Colless, and including myself as Director of Business Development in Asia, lawyer Richard Freudenstein (later Chief Operating Officer of BSkyB), finance specialist Andrew Brown, and sinologist and interpreter Laurie Smith, to meet with our *People's Daily* counterparts.

As it transpired, these counterparts included the *People's Daily* Secretary General, Zhu Xinmin, a former People's Liberation Army tank platoon commander who had been appointed to the newspaper to administer its business and commercial operations; Gu Jiawang, once a rising editorial star, who been sidelined into business development after having been found partly responsible for allowing *People's Daily* to run an editorial seen to be supportive of the student demonstrators during the lead-up to Tiananmen; and Zhang Dehua, a garrulous would-be entrepreneur working for one of the paper's myriad offshoot companies.

People's Daily had been the official newspaper of the Chinese Communist Party since 1949 and as such was seen to be the definitive source about the policies and viewpoints of the Beijing leadership. During the Cultural Revolution, which began in 1966 and ended with the arrest of the Gang of Four in 1976, *People's Daily* was eagerly sought after by both foreigners and Chinese as one of the few sources of what the government of the day was doing or thinking, as well as news of who had been purged and who had been recently elevated to a position of power. In the mid-1990s the paper could still claim a circulation of more than four million. However, *People's Daily* had to that point existed on massive government subsidies. As part of China's economic reforms, by 1994 it was under increasing pressure to find new sources of revenue which would reduce its reliance on state handouts. The paper had created the Enterprise Development Bureau to explore such options, although from what we could glean it had not been overly successful. One of its first projects had been to export a team of Chinese construction workers to Fiji to aid in the building of a three-star hotel situated near the end of the Nadi International Airport runway. The project had come to grief after the Chinese workers and local Fijian labourers had become involved in a massive brawl leading to the evacuation of the *People's Daily* contingent.

The scope of our proposed deal was, initially at least, relatively small – to publish a business news magazine with the total invested capital not expected to exceed US$5 million. However, the time involved in negotiation and discussion to formulate a means of circumventing China's tortuous media regulations was extremely arduous and dragged on for months.

The first obstacle to overcome was that according to Chinese law foreign companies were not permitted to invest or participate in the publication of any written media in China. It appeared our *People's Daily* colleagues had overlooked this small matter. As a consequence, when the first Memorandum of Understanding was produced for ratification by the Chinese authorities, it didn't actually mention the term 'publishing'. Instead, the proposed joint venture would 'enhance the economic cooperation and technical exchanges in magazine production, design and distribution, as well as other new information technologies, by adopting advanced and appropriate technology and scientific management methods, so as to raise the economic results and ensure satisfactory economic benefits for each investor'. That was acceptable and provided the means to operate in China's booming 'grey' economy – which meant that while you were not actually adhering to the regulations *per se*, you were not actually breaking them either . . . so long as you didn't push the boundaries too far.

There was, however, another obstacle – *People's Daily* had no money. The Enterprise Development Bureau's proposal was that its share of the 50 per cent capital contribution would be 'in-kind', by means of various forms of assistance and advisory services. As it turned out, *People's Daily* didn't have much of this either. It was left to me to explain to Murdoch that the reality was News Corp was getting little for its US$5 million investment other than a loose association with *People's Daily*. He shrugged his shoulders – he had just signed off on a US$20 million deal to build a studio complex in the provincial city of Tianjin, an investment that would make the *People's Daily* project look like a financial bonanza by comparison.

Tianjin had won the rights to host the 43rd World Table Tennis Championships in May 1995. Murdoch was aware that the acquisition of sporting rights in the UK had been pivotal in turning around the losses of the BSkyB satellite television network and driving up subscriptions. He believed acquiring the international rights to the Tianjin event might not only win him points with the Beijing authorities but also establish STAR TV as the premier sports network in the Asian region. Unfortunately, Tianjin had neither the facilities nor the expertise to provide a broadcast of the event to international standards.

Murdoch agreed to provide both, investing US$20 million in a 60/40 joint venture with the Tianjin Broadcasting and Television Bureau to construct four studios, including state-of-the-art edit suites, and two post-production centres. The new entity, Tianjin Golden Mainland Company, would receive the cash injection from News Corporation, while the Tianjin television authorities would provide building space and access to its existing facilities. It was a substantial investment for a week-long sporting event, but the rationale was that after the championships had finished, Golden Mainland would be in a position to provide high-end post-production facilities to the Chinese television market – facilities virtually non-existent in the country at that time – before moving into program production at some later stage.

Murdoch had indeed identified an opportunity in the market. What neither he nor the Tianjin Broadcasting and Television Bureau had done was inform Beijing – and the State Council Information Office (SCIO) in particular – about the deal. In fact, in 1994 it was not clear just who the Beijing authorities were to which News Corp was required to report. The workings of the Chinese leadership – the Communist Party especially – were still cloaked in a veil of mystery. Our understanding had always been that in relation to the television media, CCTV was the ultimate authority. Only later did we learn that CCTV was under the direction of the SCIO, which in turn reported to the Propaganda Department – an organ of the Party itself.

When the SCIO learnt of the Golden Mainland partnership it became convinced that Murdoch was trying to circumvent its authority and sneak into China, through one means or another. In the previous months, it had learnt of the media tycoon's courting of the Deng family – first Deng Rong at the lavish book launch in New York, then the visit to Australia by Deng Pufang. The Tianjin television executives were hauled to Beijing and read the riot act by the SCIO Minister Zeng Jianhui and instructed that all cooperation with the Golden Mainland partners be kept to a minimum. The SCIO also issued an edict to all state television bureaus that on no account should they enter into any commercial arrangements with the Tianjin joint venture. The SCIO would not embarrass Murdoch by ordering Golden Mainland to shut its doors immediately, but it was intent on bringing about its slow, eventual demise by strangulation.

The result was that once the World Table Tennis Championships had finished, and the 1000 international competitors left for home, the Golden Mainland facility became little more than a ghost town. Its sales executives shopped its post-production services throughout China's eastern seaboard and could not sign up a single customer. The Tianjin television officials remained singularly uncooperative, but would provide no explanation for their behaviour. Two years later, in sheer frustration, the News Corp executives inside Golden Mainland moved the bulk of the expensive post-production equipment to Beijing, in the hope that by being closer to the action the company might pick up more work. It was to no avail. The venture would be later quietly dissolved, the investment written off.

Meanwhile, the inexorable rounds of negotiation and discussion had by mid-1995 finally reached a position where the *People's Daily* joint venture – to be known as PDN (People's Daily – News) Xinren Information Technology Company Limited – could be announced to the world. After eight months of feeling our way around China's draconian media regulations, it was clear that the idea of publishing a business magazine was never going to be approved. Instead, the new company would be focusing on 'electronic publishing, online information databases, data transmission networks and digital mapping'.

But even that venture almost failed to get off the ground. The SCIO may have sent out an edict to the nation's television operators but it appeared to have failed to copy in the *People's Daily*. The first indication that there might be a problem occurred on the evening before the scheduled joint press conference to announce the venture. Secretary General Zhu Xinmin was two hours late for a meeting with Malcolm Colless and myself to sign off on the wording of the intended press release. When he finally arrived the former tank commander was pale and nervous. He had just been on the end of an enormous lambasting from his superior, *People's Daily* President Shao Huaze, who had in turn been called to the offices of the powerful Propaganda Department to issue a personal explanation to Ding Guangen himself.

One of the editors-in-chief, having sighted the proposed press release, had seen fit to send on a copy to the SCIO, where Minister Zeng Jianhui was mortified. Not only had Murdoch managed to out-manoeuvre his office again, this time it was not just with some provincial television operator, but one of the Communist Party's most revered institutions, *People's Daily*. Zeng had notified Ding, and the Propaganda Chief had hauled in Shao, who had just finished berating his Secretary General.

Zhu sat before us in the hotel lobby of the China World Hotel, barely able to speak. He stammered out something about there being a problem and that perhaps it would be best to cancel the proposed press conference. Colless and I argued against it on the basis that it would be a huge loss of face to all concerned. We suggested we could water down the press release and talk of merely 'cooperation' and 'information technology', and shy away from any discussion of the media. Zhu nodded, excused himself and left for another meeting with the SCIO. He returned just before midnight and informed us that the press conference could proceed but stressed the message from Murdoch must be that this 'was a strategic relationship based on cooperation and mutual recognition of the qualities each side brought to the venture'. He said it also should be stressed that News Corporation would respect China's 'laws, regulations and moral values'.

The announcement of the joint venture received worldwide media coverage with most correspondents, much to the chagrin of the SCIO, suggesting the deal represented a 'thaw in the frosty relationship between Murdoch and China'. The truth was anything but. Our colleagues warned us it would be a good time to leave Beijing – indeed, to leave China – for a while.

'It's a very hot issue, just now. Very hot,' they said. 'Better you leave for a few weeks and return when things have cooled down.'

The great Chinese warrior strategist Sun Tzu noted in his much-quoted treatise *The Art of War* that the 'general is skilful in attack whose enemy knows not what to defend, and is skilful in defence whose enemy does not know what to attack'. The SCIO could be forgiven for thinking that Murdoch had become a student of the warrior general himself. From the SCIO's point of view, Murdoch's attacks on its defences could never be predicted; he simply kept on coming at the Great Wall no matter what was done to deflect his assaults. It was concerned that sooner or later he would break through. The SCIO was in desperate need of a strategy that would allow them to control Murdoch's entry into China; an entry that would be at its timing and its pace.

The answer was about to walk in the door.

5

Phoenix Rising

The stocky, bespectacled Chinese property developer with the Belize passport who ambled through the front door of STAR TV's swish Hong Kong harbour-front offices was a far cry from the normal businessmen who sat down at the negotiating table with one of the most powerful men in the world. Rupert Murdoch was used to crossing swords with world leaders and billionaires, tycoons and tyrants, but an upstart mystery millionaire demanding a half share of a joint venture television channel in China was quite something else.

Liu Changle, at 1.9 metres and nearly 100 kilograms, was a big man with even bigger ambitions. He wanted to be the Rupert Murdoch of Chinese-language television with a network that spread around the world. Furthermore, he uttered as he lowered his considerable bulk into one of the plush armchairs in the STAR TV executive office, he wanted to kick-start his ambitious plans via a joint venture in China with Murdoch himself. Liu had no shortage of front.

By the northern autumn of 1995, Murdoch was becoming increasingly frustrated at his failure to breach the Great Wall the Chinese authorities had erected to prevent him gaining access to the country's potentially lucrative satellite pay television market. His courting of Paramount Leader Deng Xiaoping's family had come to naught. His overtures to CCTV for cooperation had been politely rejected. Murdoch remained firmly on the blacklist, even refused permission to meet the very authorities whose forgiveness he required.

Murdoch had consulted fellow tycoons – billionaire businessmen like Li Ka-shing and Robert Kwok, both of whom were making new fortunes investing in China's booming economy and were known to have close contacts at the highest levels of the Chinese leadership. Neither could offer much in the way of solace other than to suggest he 'persist and persist until finally something gave'. Persistence was never Murdoch's weak suit; it was patience he could lack.

In Hong Kong, Gary Davey was midway through the second year of his term as STAR TV Chief Executive, a significant achievement given both his predecessors had lasted but a few months in the job. Davey was a savvy operator who had already pruned US$20 million off the broadcaster's US$100 million loss the previous year, closed a welter of programming and distribution agreements, and split STAR TV's satellite signal into two separate beams, one aimed primarily at China and the second at India, its two largest markets. There had also been progress in establishing pay TV operations in the Philippines and Taiwan – although collecting monies from the Taipei Triad gangs who ran the majority of the cable networks would later prove something of a challenge.

But China, potentially the most lucrative of all the markets, remained tantalisingly out of reach. Despite the tens of thousands of entrepreneurial cable operators surreptitiously downloading the STAR TV signal and distributing it across the nation to tens of millions of subscribers, Murdoch was unable to collect a single cent in return. Advertisers, well aware that STAR TV was 'on the nose' with the Beijing leadership, stayed away in droves for fear of being tainted by the Murdoch brush. STAR TV was a business without a revenue stream.

Davey's critical task, then, was to find a crack in China's Great Wall. He was new to Asia and hence to China, but had played a pivotal role in turning around the ruinous losses of Murdoch's BSkyB operations in the United Kingdom. Despite his extraordinary energy and unswerving optimism, STAR TV was proving a bigger challenge than anything he had come up against at BSkyB. To make matters worse, Murdoch was literally on the telephone every other day seeking news of progress.

The problem was knowing where to start. There was no end of consultants, entrepreneurs, would-be media magnates and carpet-baggers coming through Davey's door with any number of proposals to crack the market. For the most part, Davey would listen with feigned interest before showing them the door. Of all the promoters who came to STAR TV, the one who seemed least likely to be able to offer anything of substance was a Chinese real estate developer and part-time oil trader with a Belize passport and a passion for fine food and red wine.

When Liu Changle turned up at the STAR TV office he was a complete unknown. He had never appeared on the radar of potential partners in China and, as far as any of us could ascertain, he had no history of having been involved in satellite pay television. Yet, as Davey would later recall, after a two-hour meeting it was clear Liu knew more about News Corporation's operations around the world and its ambitions in China than anybody – with the possible exception of Murdoch himself. Davey was deeply impressed by Liu's understanding of both News Corp and the Chinese regulatory environment. But who was he?

Liu was very circumspect about his background, at least initially. What we did uncover was that he had been the child of relatively senior Communist Party officials and had grown up in reasonable comfort until the Cultural Revolution in the 1960s. Like so many of his contemporaries, he watched from the sidelines as his parents were humiliated and paraded through the streets of Lanzhou, the capital of one of China's western provinces. At nineteen, Liu joined the People's Liberation Army (PLA).

Liu would later tell me he had originally been assigned to a road-works unit but in his spare time would write articles on Communist ideology for the army newspapers, which whetted his appetite for journalism. After the Cultural Revolution, Liu joined the Communist Party and was given a job in the Propaganda Department of the Central People's Radio Station.

His big break apparently came in the mid-1980s, when Liu was assigned to accompany Yang Shangkun, then Deputy to Paramount Leader Deng Xiaoping and Vice Chairman of the powerful Central Military Commission, on a trip to the United States. The two are thought to have struck up a particular friendship and certainly Liu's career started to blossom. By 1987 he had attained the rank of colonel and was managing one of the army's Beijing radio stations.

But from this time Liu's history becomes a little murky. Around the end of 1987, Liu quit the PLA, acquired the Belize passport, left the country and ended up variously in Houston, Singapore and Hong Kong working as a private oil trader. China's booming economy was full of opportunities for astute operators like Liu, especially if you had powerful connections in the military and particularly if those connections had access to cheap, subsidised fuel during the oil crisis of 1990.

I was told Liu was able to use his influential PLA relationships to acquire tanker-loads of cheap Chinese crude oil, have it refined in Singapore and then sell it on the international market for a very healthy profit. Whatever the source of Liu's rapid accumulation of wealth, he remained extremely reticent to discuss it. But by the time he turned up at STAR TV ready to talk business with Rupert Murdoch, Liu was by Chinese standards a very wealthy man. He was maintaining homes in Beijing, Hong Kong and California, and sent his twin daughters to college in the United States. His Hong Kong-registered company, Carefree Development Limited, had become a substantial property developer in China, as well as winning lucrative concessions to operate a number of major tollways.

Liu's proposition to Murdoch was for the establishment of a Chinese-language entertainment channel that would be jointly owned by News Corp and his own Asia Today media company. Liu also suggested that it would help the duo's cause if they were to gift the powerful CCTV organisation a 10 per cent stake in the new business venture. He was offering to use his high-level *guanxi* in Beijing to have carriage of the channel officially approved, at least in some provinces of China. Murdoch, in return, was to put up the bulk of the cash, pull his existing Chinese-language channel off the air and cede total editorial control to Liu, who would be the Chief Executive of the venture – to be christened Phoenix.

Murdoch was going to take a lot of persuading. For a start, the deal broke his golden rule: Never own anything you don't control. He also remained unconvinced that Liu had the connections to get the landing rights approval that to date had been denied to Murdoch despite his furious courting of the leadership and the significant investments he had made. There was also the question of the former Colonel's links to the PLA and how a joint venture between News Corp and the army that just a few years earlier had brutally crushed a popular uprising in Tiananmen Square might be perceived in the wider world outside China.

Liu, however, had already astutely cultivated the key decision makers in Beijing – the National Security Bureau and the Propaganda Department – before making his approach to Davey at STAR TV. The two government departments had been tasked with monitoring and controlling Murdoch's advance in China and up to this point they had been sorely tested. Liu's plan, if Murdoch gave it his assent, would provide some respite in that it would serve to sate the media tycoon's appetite for a while, and allow the Beijing authorities the opportunity to observe News Corp's intentions up close, yet all the while have a trusted hand on the editorial helm. It was akin to having one of their own inside the enemy camp.

Davey had an exceedingly difficult time getting Murdoch across the line on the deal. The STAR TV CEO argued that while it may not have been the best deal, it was the only deal on the table. There was little indication of any thaw in the relationship with Beijing, and at least the Phoenix channel would allow News Corp to prove its credentials. When Murdoch asked my advice, I told him I was concerned that Liu was a 'stalking horse' for the Beijing authorities, and that I thought we were giving up an awful lot at the risk of damaging News Corp's reputation if it got out that we were in bed with the PLA.

It wasn't the PLA. A few weeks later, in December 1995, the negotiations between the two parties had reached a point where a decision needed to be made one way or another. Davey told Liu that while there had been a lot of talk up to that point about the latter's *guanxi* in Beijing he had yet to show his hand. Liu responded with an invitation to a cocktail party to be hosted by his company, Carefree Development, in a state guesthouse outside of Beijing.

Present was the STAR TV Deputy Chairman, Lachlan Murdoch, Davey and a gaggle of STAR TV executives, as well as Liu and his entourage of minders. True to his word, Liu had turned out an impressive array of senior Chinese government officials, including Minister Zeng Jianhui from the SCIO and Li Bing, whose sole role in life was to keep an eye on News Corp's Chinese activities. But the guest of honour was one Luo Gan, whose business card read 'member of the Standing Committee of the Communist Party of China (CPC) Central Committee Political Bureau and the Secretary of the Political and Legislative Affairs Committee of the CPC Central Committee'. Luo was in fact the feared head of the National Security Bureau – China's top official in charge of all security matters.

It was a convivial evening, marked by warm speeches about 'mutual cooperation and respect', a good many toasts of maotai rice spirits and red wine. Toward the end of the evening Luo walked up behind where Davey and Liu had been chatting amicably and put a firm hand on the scruff of each man's neck.

'Now,' he said, pulling the men's heads together and not releasing his firm grip on their necks, 'you are going to have to get together and make this work.'

The message was clear. If Murdoch wished to enter China officially, Phoenix was indeed the route which he should go down. This was not a courtship but a shotgun wedding.

The Phoenix Chinese Channel launched just over three months later, on 31 March 1996, and it had a profound effect upon the Chinese television industry landscape. CCTV was still the nation's dominant broadcaster and its programming was austere and straight-laced news bulletins delivered in deadpan monotones, the bulk of its general entertainment made up of historical dramas with a strong ideological tinge or gala concerts of performing cultural troupes. Whatever else he was, Liu was a canny programmer who, with Murdoch's backing, set about giving the Chinese a taste of contemporary television broadcasting.

Phoenix launched with spectacular animated graphics, diversified programming that included modern drama, talk shows, pop music and, previously unheard of in China, on-air personalities. Although he was careful in the early days to run a series of flattering shows about Paramount Leader Deng Xiaoping, carefully scripted so as not to show up new leader Jiang Zemin, and he avoided controversial subjects such as Tiananmen Square, Liu gradually added news programs, then Western-style chat shows and current affairs programming, formats never before seen on state-run television.

Borrowing heavily from the US experience, Phoenix began broadcasting a mix of productions from China and abroad, including sports, music and infotainment shows like *Good Morning China*, *Phoenix Afternoon Express*, *Phoenix Tonight*, *Passion On China*, *The Asian Journal* and *Newsline*.

Unlike the state-owned broadcasters, Phoenix had no obligation to serve all the people, all the time. Liu's programming was very much targeted at China's new aspirational class of higher income earners and professionals. By 1999 the station was the highest-rating foreign television channel in the country and the surveys showed it had a brand awareness equal to that of McDonald's and General Motors.

Although Phoenix still had no official carriage beyond hotels rated three-star and above, official compounds and international residential areas, it was clear that the Chinese leadership had become regular viewers. In March 1998, in his inaugural press conference as the newly appointed Premier, Zhu Rongji endorsed the channel, telling one of its reporters during a televised news conference that he was a fan. It was official endorsement of an unofficial television channel.

CCTV, we would learn, received an official rebuke from the Politburo demanding that it lift its presentation and performance standards, which it promptly did by investing massive amounts of capital in new on-air graphics technology, presentation and play-out equipment. Everything that Phoenix did was imitated by the national broadcaster and the major provincial television stations in Shanghai and Guangdong. China's moribund television industry had been galvanised into action.

More choice meant more viewers and more advertising. Although Phoenix would lose around US$53 million during its first three years of operation, its advertising revenues soon surpassed that of all other STAR TV channels combined. For all its success, however, Murdoch was never completely happy with the Phoenix deal. He never saw himself as a venture capitalist or silent partner in any business deal. Murdoch always demanded control of any venture he invested in, and in Phoenix he did not have that control. Worse, Liu's not inconsiderable ego was ensuring that he, not Murdoch, was getting much of the credit for the success.

The Chinese authorities, particularly the SCIO, were perplexed by Murdoch's seeming lack of gratitude. They thought they had given him a significant break — no other foreign media company had been given approval (tacit though it was) to broadcast into China. Yet Murdoch continued to agitate for an open skies regime that would allow him unfettered access to the living rooms of China. For Murdoch, it was a start. He'd helped turn the Chinese television industry on its head and set it on the path to modernisation. But it was still not enough — it was never enough.

6

ChinaByte

It was apt, perhaps, given News Corporation's missteps in China, that the site of its first official presence in downtown Beijing was on the fourteenth floor of a city office building. Fourteen is considered to be one of the unluckiest numbers in Chinese culture, and most office and apartment buildings judiciously avoid ever having a fourteenth floor. Fourteen in Mandarin (*shi si*) can sound like the equivalent of 'ten die'. Sometimes the number is also expressed as 'one-four' (*yi si*), which can sound a lot like 'want to die'. Not particularly auspicious as far as the Chinese were concerned.

It probably explained both the mirth of the Chinese bureaucrats when reading our business cards and also why the entire floor was available at a significantly discounted rate compared to other space in the building.

But having made our bed with the Communist Party mouthpiece, *People's Daily*, we now had to lie in it. Rupert Murdoch had never walked away from a challenge, and while the *People's Daily*/News Corp joint venture PDN was certainly neither the most important nor the most expensive step the company had taken into uncharted territory, it was nevertheless going to be a showcase of 'cooperation and mutual benefit' that could be held up in front of the Chinese leadership as a precursor to bigger and better things in the future. The result of that unlikely union was that the PDN Xinren Information Technology Company Limited opened for business in January of 1996.

To understand the impact of the internet in China it needs to be remembered that since its coming to power in 1949 the Chinese Communist Party had maintained an absolute iron-fisted control over all aspects of the media. Every word that was printed, transmitted or broadcast was first vetted by some anonymous cadres somewhere deep in the extraordinary labyrinth that was the vast and all-powerful Propaganda Department. Every book published, every film produced, every report of events within and outside of China, required the imprimatur of the state. Now the internet threatened to put an end to the absolute control the Party had to date exercised over the ebb and flow of information throughout the country. But the conundrum for the Party was the recognition that without access to the 'information superhighway' China's development would fall far beyond that of the West. It understood that it needed to open the door to the internet – the question was how far.

The Chinese leadership was at odds over whether to allow public access to the newfangled internet or not. There were endless debates in the official media about its worth and the unbridled dangers of allowing Chinese youth access to the decadence and pornography of Western culture. However, from mid-1995 on, individuals with sufficient funds were able to purchase internet accounts from CHINANET, the country's first commercial Internet Service Provider, which was operated by the government via the Ministry of Post and Telecommunications (MPT). At first, the take-up was relatively modest as the web was still a very recent phenomenon, little known outside the hallowed corridors of China's academic institutions, although the Chinese domestic media was starting to report on its surging popularity in the Western world at some length. Its growth in China was largely promulgated by returning Chinese students who had firsthand experience of the web and email while studying at international institutions abroad, and who convincingly argued that the nation could not afford to be cut off from this new information gateway.

But within a year of easing the door open a crack, the Beijing leadership was moving to slam it shut again. The move to allow individual internet accounts unleashed an extraordinary wave of excitement, energy and enlightenment across China, particularly in the university campuses and urban areas. A new generation of young Chinese, having seen glimpses of the outside world via the advent of satellite television, were now eagerly seeking access to a personal uncensored window into the world beyond. In 1995 the best official estimates were that there were around 250 000 Chinese connecting to the internet across the whole of the country. By the end of 1996, when young Chinese entrepreneur Edward Zeng opened the doors of Beijing's first internet café, the numbers had already reached a million and were doubling every six months. (By 2000 there would be some 10 million online users in China and as of 2007 the number was 137 million, according to the China Internet Network Information Centre, and includes more than 90.7 million broadband subscribers.)

This brief flurry of unchecked, uncensored internet access came to an abrupt close by the end of December 1995. While the ageing Chinese leadership was largely considered barely computer literate, the Propaganda Department's Ding Guangen was a notable exception. Our *People's Daily* colleagues told us that Ding had installed Microsoft's Windows 95 and Internet Explorer on his home computer earlier that month to understand what all the fuss was about. He had begun browsing the web. It was during these home browsing sessions that Comrade Ding had stumbled on some pornographic websites, as well as those of several Chinese dissident groups which carried tirades against the Chinese leadership and newsletters which were providing uncensored accounts of protests by disgruntled workers in the provinces.

Unfortunately for the PDN Xinren joint venture, the Propaganda Chief's viewing habits had invoked the expected hard-line response from the authorities. The day we formally commenced operations, in the first week of January 1996, the government called for a crackdown on the internet to 'rid the country of unwanted pornography and detrimental information'. Days later the State Council announced that no more international internet gateways would be permitted to link to the outside world and new user registration would be postponed indefinitely.

On 23 January Premier Li Peng detailed new rules governing internet operations. As an Internet Content Provider, PDN Xinren was required to immediately sign an undertaking that we would not engage in activities at the expense of state security; that we would not produce, retrieve, duplicate or spread information that might hinder public order; and that we acknowledge that pornography was explicitly banned. Our business plan was looking decidedly sick.

On 14 February the powerful Ministry of Public Security issued a circular requiring all internet users to register with them within thirty days. It was not exactly an auspicious beginning for an internet start-up, but fortunately such was the exponential growth spurt in people connecting to the internet that the government bureaucracy hardly had time to stay abreast of the newly promulgated laws and regulations.

As general manager of the new joint venture company, I was required to make my way down to the local office of the Ministry of Public Security to register it. The officer in charge not only had no knowledge of the new rules requiring such registration, he had absolutely no comprehension of what we were talking about, and kept shrugging his shoulders and rolling his eyes despite the best efforts of myself and my interpreter.

Finally, somewhat exasperated, I suggested the interpreter try the Chinese translation of 'information superhighway' instead of 'internet'. The Public Security Officer's face lit up, he came out from behind the counter, gripped me by the elbow and led me to the door and pointed across the road to the building marked 'Traffic Police'. Despite my protestations, he insisted it was not Public Security I needed to register with, but the officers of the Highway Patrol division. Just as well I had a Chinese driving licence.

The product of the PDN joint venture was to be a technology news and information website – www.chinabyte.com, or more simply, ChinaByte. Getting it started proved a little more challenging than we anticipated, despite the enormous resources that News Corp could throw at it. The venture's first office was a disused school classroom in the dustier end of the *People's Daily* compound. It had just a single power point to run our computer equipment, no airconditioning to deal with Beijing's sweltering summer heat, and windows that failed to close and keep out the freezing cold winter winds. Our business planning sessions were often interrupted by students playing football on the concrete common area outside the room's windows during breaks from class.

By mid-1996 the joint venture had moved to new offices on the fourteenth floor of a refurbished office building behind Beijing's China World Hotel. It was an improvement on the disused classroom but still presented numerous challenges. The day after we completed the fit-out, officers from the local fire department turned up and insisted we would require a two-metre fire corridor down the centre of the office, even though they had previously approved all the plans. After a 'donation' to the fire department's workers fund, they settled for an emergency exit door in our conference room – which was kept locked, of course. The building's airconditioning couldn't cope with the heat generated by our computer servers and so we had to bring in portable airconditioners attached to open windows to pump additional cool air into our working space, lest the staff and the servers expire in the heat. Office space in Beijing in 1996 was at a premium and we were paying rent which was the equivalent to Manhattan or the Ginza district of Tokyo. My apartment – a modest two-bedroom affair in nearby Jianguomenwai Avenue – was costing in excess of US$10 500 a month. Our office and accommodation costs were fast exceeding our entire operating budget for the year.

For the good part of its first year of operation, PDN Xinren was an internet company without an internet connection. It took some seven months and an endless round of incentive payments to various officials at the Ministry of Post and Telecommunication to provide a line, payments to another department to lay the cable, and still further inducements to have someone actually connect it to the PDN office. In the end we were the proud 'owners' of a 28k dedicated connection to the internet, for which we were required to pay some US$22 000 a month in rent. It was a sum so ridiculous – and non-negotiable – that it gave rise to rumours that Rupert Murdoch was actually subsidising the growth of the internet across the whole of China.

It was against this background that Murdoch and *People's Daily* had come together to launch what would be one of the first commercial web content sites in China. Our staff of thirty, made up largely of local fresh-faced university graduates in their early to mid-twenties, were absolutely awestruck by the world they found at the end of a URL address. They would sit spellbound in front of the computer screens for upwards of sixteen hours a day. Many of them began to sleep overnight in the office rather than go home, a fact that became all too apparent when on a visit to the PDN office Murdoch pulled out a chair in the conference room to be confronted with a pair of our graphic artist's dirty underpants. He'd been sleeping under the conference table for more than a month.

The full magnitude of what we were a part of during those early days of Murdoch's China internet adventure was brought home one Saturday afternoon in Beijing when I let myself into the normally closed PDN office to catch up on some paperwork. At a computer terminal sat one of the young female staffers, beside an older man who she introduced as her father. She was giving him a tour of the internet and its resources. He had, I later learnt, been a highly regarded biochemist of international standing when the Cultural Revolution intervened and he had been packed off to work in the rice fields of rural western China. His textbooks were burnt and his laboratory smashed, and he spent ten years away from any semblance of academia. Unable to keep pace with bioscience developments in the West, his career and reputation had quietly faded into oblivion.

An hour later there was a tap at my office door. Miss Wan asked if it was okay for her father to come in and say a few words. The old man gripped my wrist with both his hands and clung on. There were tears rolling down his cheeks.

'It is as though my whole life has been lived in a darkened room,' he said. 'And now a light has been turned on. Thank you. Thank you.' With that he turned and walked towards the office door, his head still rocking from side to side as if in disbelief at all he'd seen.

Rupert, on the other hand, was still very much an internet sceptic in 1996, dismissing it as little more than a passing fad. He simply couldn't see how websites would be able to monetise their content. Although he would later have a change of mind, launching a massive buying spree of internet properties across the world (just months before the tech bubble burst in 2000), in terms of China his mind was still very much focused on his main game – landing rights for the STAR TV network.

Fortunately, Lachlan Murdoch, then the recently appointed CEO of News Limited (Australia), was named a director of the PDN Xinren joint venture company. Lachlan had himself recently appointed one of his closest American school and rock-climbing buddies, Zeb Rice, to establish a small interactive operation supporting News Limited's Australian newspapers. Rice had an impeccable US Democratic Party heritage. His mother, Kathleen Brown, a Senior Vice President with Citibank, had been an unsuccessful 1994 Democrat candidate for governor of California. Pursuing California's highest political office was a family trait – his uncle, Jerry Brown, and grandfather, Pat Brown, had both been two-term governors of the state, as well as failed US presidential candidates. Lachlan appointed Rice as technical adviser to the up-and-coming ChinaByte site. Odd it was that this scion of US West Coast liberalism found himself working alongside card-carrying members of China's Communist Party.

Rice, along with News Limited director Malcolm Colless, made regular visits from Sydney to Beijing to check on the progress of joint venture. On one occasion, Lachlan accompanied the team from Australia for a tour of the new PDN facility and a motivational speech to the young Chinese staffers. Afterwards, a rather boisterous bonding session with the staff and management at a nearby Sichuan restaurant involved a great deal of toasting with the powerful local maotai rice wine. Towards the end of the evening, our Chinese guests were dumbfounded as the heir to the Murdoch empire and his buddy Rice indulged in a climbing contest around the restaurant's walls. Each had to complete a circumnavigation of the room without touching the floor. Rice claimed victory after a beam in the roof appeared to fail under the younger Murdoch's weight, sending him crashing to the floor. There was thunderous applause all round. One can only imagine what Ding Guangen and the apparatchiks in the Propaganda Department would make of the reports of the evening's proceedings they received the following day. We were always aware that, as News Corporation executives, we were followed and our phones tapped.

It was Rice's first experience of Asia and he was clearly fascinated by the culture and enthused by the PDN Xinren project, which helped garner valuable support back at head office where questions were increasingly being asked about where the money was going and the overall value of the project in the scheme of Murdoch's China ambitions. Rice was well-connected to the internet community in the US, and through his contacts we were able to attract some talented young web producers, developers and graphic artists out of New York to help train the local staff. But it was his mother's banking connections that led to an invitation from one of China's new banking czars for Rice and me to represent News Corp at a private dinner where we were to confront one end of the full gamut of Chinese cuisine.

Keen to impress, our host ushered us into a private room at a swank Chinese restaurant specialising in exotic dishes. When the first dish arrived and was set down in front of us we were invited to partake of what looked like whole mushroom soup. I spooned a mushroom into my mouth and bit down, then stopped. I could see Rice had the very same reaction. This was the toughest, weirdest-tasting mushroom I had ever come across. Out of the corner of my eye, I saw the interpreter sitting on my left side toy with her serving, pick up the dinner menu, to peruse it and then politely push the dish away. I discreetly spat my 'mushroom' back into the spoon and gently lowered it into the bowl.

'What is that?' I inquired in an aside to the interpreter.

'I think the translation is, "sphincter of male suckling pig",' she replied.

'Pig's arse?' I spluttered. Turning mine over in the dish, I could then clearly see she was correct. 'I thought it was a mushroom!'

'Yes,' she said. 'An upside-down sphincter surely looks like the underside of a mushroom. One should always check.'

ChinaByte was launched on 17 January 1997 to considerable local fanfare in Beijing and a good deal of international media coverage. During the first week of going live it was receiving 2500 visits a day – by year's end it was getting 2.5 million hits a month, making it the most popular IT site in China. However, like a lot of websites in the early days of the first internet revo-lution, it struggled with revenue from advertising banner sales and continued to require hefty financial input from News Corp to keep it afloat.

By late 1999, when Rupert Murdoch belatedly decided News Corp needed an internet strategy and went on a US$1 billion investment splurge on web ventures, ChinaByte and PDN didn't figure.

News Corp formed the venture capital company ePartners in April 1999, with US$300 million to invest in the internet, interactive television and wireless communication. Its first significant investment was a 50 per cent interest in eVentures, jointly funded with Japan's Softbank. Eighteen months later, eVentures folded, a victim of the burst internet bubble.

Murdoch followed with a US$700 million bet on Healtheon/WebMD, giving Healtheon 50 per cent of his Health Network cable channel as part of the deal. A year later, the cooperation between the two companies was basically canned. News Corp took a US$200 million non-cash charge in the fourth quarter of 2000 and clawed back 100 per cent ownership of the Health Network.

James Murdoch, with the assistance of his new stepmother, Wendi Deng, went on a buying spree across Asia, spending some US$120 million on stakes in about twenty dotcoms across China and India, including a minority stake in Chinese internet service provider Netease, and the Chinese language portal renren. Having bought in at the top of the market, News Corp had divested virtually all of its China internet holdings by 2002 at a significant loss.

Although at the forefront of China's internet revolution, China-Byte had also fallen out of favour, despite it having developed one of the country's earliest Chinese-language search engines in Cseek.com and a popular entertainment site, Joyday.com. Murdoch had lost faith in China and the internet. The tech bubble had burst and News Corp was in full retreat from the internet.

By April 2001, News Corp had virtually divested itself of China-Byte, allowing it to be merged with rival IT website yesky.com. In doing so, Murdoch gave up his foothold in the fastest-growing internet market in the world.

ChinaByte not only survived the dotcom bust – and being dumped by Murdoch – but went on to flourish.

According to a 2006 industry association survey of internet businesses in China, ChinaByte was ranked as the number one brand among IT-related internet sites. The Chinese internet research company iResearch (www.iresearch.com.cn) ranked ChinaByte number one among Chinese IT-related internet sites in terms of advertising volume (and number nine among all Chinese internet sites). In addition, ChinaByte is now one of the largest providers of information content and games to cellular phone users in China, including two of the country's largest mobile phone corporations, China Mobile and China Unicom. In June 2006, Japanese digital media publishing group Impress Holdings paid US$10 million for a 20 per cent stake in ChinaByte and plans to list the company on the NASDAQ exchange in 2008.

Having walked away from ChinaByte, there was some irony in News Corp's announcement in late 2006 that it would sell a 20 per cent stake in its Phoenix Television channel to China Mobile as part of an 'alliance with China Mobile to provide media content to China's 480 million mobile phone users'. For a man often credited with the ability to see around corners, ChinaByte proved Murdoch was by no means infallible.

7

Accidental Heroes

Acurmudgeonly, dour bunch, the collected editors-in-chief of *People's Daily* had assembled in the fourteenth-floor office of the PDN Xinren joint venture, where we were constructing our proposed ChinaByte website, to see for themselves just what this internet business was all about.

There were eight of them in total, mostly aged in their late fifties or early sixties, and dressed in a mixture of dark grey Western business suits or the Mao jacket favoured by the late Paramount Leader, Deng Xiaoping. A whiff of disdain emanated from the group. After all, they were within the confines of the greatest of all capitalist roaders – 'Mur-Dock' – and none of them looked particularly happy to be there. You could sense they were reluctant to touch anything lest some consumerist bacteria infect them, leaving them forever tainted.

People's Daily was the strangest of beasts. The official mouthpiece of the all-powerful Chinese Communist Party (CCP), its editorials and musings were regarded as the 'words of God' handed down from above. What appeared in *People's Daily* had been pre-ordained and therefore represented an insight into the leadership's thinking – or more importantly, an inkling of the machinations occurring behind the guarded high walls of Zhongnanhai, the secretive complex on the western side of the Forbidden City which was home to China's leadership elite.

But it was never just the words in the newspaper, which even in the early 1990s retained a circulation of some four million, but the placement of stories and the positioning of photographs and who was in them that were minutely examined by China-watchers the world over. Even the size of an official's image or its placement on the page might signify whether his particular star was on the wax or wane. So important was this concept of placement, it was explained to us, that one of the editors-in-chief's sole responsibilities was to measure each individual photograph to ensure it was neither too small nor too large, and not placed too high or too low on the page as befitting the official's rank of the day.

A photograph placed prominently above the paper fold was a sure sign that a particular minister or cadre was enjoying the full support of the CCP leadership. Being photographed with President Jiang Zemin was a signal that you had been welcomed into the elite inner sanctum of trusted compatriots. By the same token, an official who picked up the morning edition of *People's Daily* and realised their photograph had dramatically been downsized – or worse, they had been airbrushed out of an official portrait – knew their use-by date was fast approaching.

So it was that every minister, cadre, public servant, diplomat and China-watcher scoured every edition of *People's Daily* for some sign, some indicator of who was in, who was out and sometimes who had been out but was now being rehabilitated.

Once, in a rare private moment with the suave, white-haired President of *People's Daily*, Shao Huaze – a former army general whose interest in Chinese poetry and practice of calligraphy belied his hard-line ideological bent – I inquired about the most memorable moments in his long career.

'Without doubt,' he said, 'it was the morning of March 1973, when I picked up a copy of the *People's Daily* and there was a photograph of the leadership following a banquet given in honour of Prince Norodom Sihanouk of Kampuchea at the Sichuan Restaurant (now the elite China Club) in Xi Rong Xian Lane, near the Forbidden City.

'In the corner of the photograph was the unmistakable figure of Comrade Deng. It was the first indication that he was back, having been stripped of all his posts during the Cultural Revolution and banished to a tractor factory in the far west.

'I cried. *Cried*. Because I knew that now Comrade Deng was back, the suffering would end, the madness would stop and things would change for the better.'

But even in the mid-1990s those seeking the latest insights into the thinking of the Chinese leadership had to wait for a mail-delivered, or at best air-freighted, copy of *People's Daily*, which meant that even China's own diplomats were days or even weeks behind their mainland counterparts. In 1995, in production terms *People's Daily* was a weird mixture of ancient and modern. There were still relatively few computers available to staff and the composition of the pages prior to printing was still largely done by hand. Highly skilled compositors would sit at a table containing a single page of the morning edition. Because of the complexity of Chinese characters – even utilising the simplified versions – there were trays containing hundreds upon hundreds of characters from which the compositor would select a single slug to place on the page. Little wonder the deadline for the next day's edition was two in the afternoon. After each page was completed, a dozen galley proofs would be made and each checked and re-checked by editors, words corrected, photographs measured, nuances and political tone all signed off by the various editors-in-chief, before finally going to press.

On the other hand, *People's Daily* possessed one of the most sophisticated satellite processing and transmission systems anywhere in the world. Not even *The New York Times* could match the scale and sophistication of the *People's Daily*'s remote publishing operation. Each page of the next day's edition was scanned and then up-linked to the newspaper's dedicated satellite transponder where the signal was re-transmitted to some twenty-three printing plants across China, thereby allowing the paper to be printed and distributed on the same day in every major national centre.

With a circulation then of some 3.5 million, it was among the highest-selling newspapers in the world, albeit – given its rather tedious tone – one of the few whose circulation possibly exceeded its readership.

In each city, massive MAN Roland printing presses, imported from Germany at great cost and the equivalent of or better than those of any major Western publishing giant, were poised and ready to roll off hundreds of thousands of copies of the morning edition. And in each centre there were back-up presses, many of them never used but there as a guarantee that there would never be a day when *People's Daily* did not hit the streets of China.

The sprawling *People's Daily* (PD) compound in Jintaixi Road, in Beijing's Chaoyang District, was not only home to thousands of employees who lived on the premises, but a warehouse of every available printing press – monster monotype machines, Goss colour presses and heatset machines, many still in their wrapping. PD had plans to become a major printing and publishing house for all of China but somehow had managed to purchase more presses than it had work for.

It was also apparent that PD's enthusiasm for new machines

was not always matched by the energy required to maintain them. One of Murdoch's ideas had been to look at forming a separate joint venture with PD to establish a printing operation capable of producing high-quality, glossy magazine titles for the China market. A series of discussions had been held and finally it was agreed that a technical team from Australia would come to Beijing to assist our Chinese counterparts with a particularly troublesome colour press that was failing to provide an acceptable print quality, despite being just a year or so old. The Australian technical team duly observed while the presses ran and were themselves at a loss to explain the mottled, washed-out result that ensued.

'Tell you what,' said a visiting Australian printer. 'When you've finished the run and washed the rollers, we'll take a closer look.'

'What do you mean, "wash the rollers"?' came the incredulous reply from his Chinese counterpart. 'What is "wash rollers"?'

That particular venture never did get off the ground.

There was little doubt that PD had the domestic market well and truly covered. The challenge was how it might meet the needs of the tens of thousands of China-watchers, plus the vast Chinese diaspora around the world who hungered for news and information from the venerable official CCP but had to wait days and weeks before it reached their doorsteps.

So it was that I sowed the seed with President Shao and his erstwhile offsider, General Secretary Zhu Xinmin, that perhaps an internet edition of *People's Daily* might present a viable solution.

It was they who encouraged, cajoled, pushed and prodded the senior cadres of the newspaper to venture outside the Chaoyang compound to visit the PDN office, for a firsthand look at the 'information superhighway', as it was then known.

At the time there was a struggle within the ruling elite about the whole internet phenomenon. The hard-line conservatives, not surprisingly led by Premier Li Peng and Propaganda Department head Ding Guangen, were totally opposed to allowing the public unfettered access to uncontrolled and uncensored information. Control of the media – the ebb and flow of information to the greater populace – was a paramount tenet of the CCP doctrine. The Propaganda Department in 1995 was still one of the most powerful offices of power and influence in China. Ding, handpicked by Deng Xiaoping himself, exercised an iron-fist rule of all China's media, as well as being responsible for how China was presented to the outside world.

On the other side was Vice Premier Zhu Rongji, the pragmatic economic czar, who felt China could not ignore the information flows offered by the internet as the country struggled to come to terms with competing in a global economy. President Jiang Zemin was thought to be sitting on the fence, not yet convinced one way or the other, but his background in electrical engineering was thought to have made him at least alert to the positive potential of an information superhighway.

For those of us involved in China's nascent internet industry at the time, the reading of the tea-leaves suggested the government was about to slam the shutters on the internet and restrict it to all but a few authorised academics and military personnel. The conservative old guard had maintained a convincing line about protecting Chinese virtue from the decadent pornography and unadulterated consumerism of the Western world. There were reports of draconian legislation being prepared to restrict access, limit gateways and maintain the status quo of total control.

On the fourteenth floor at PDN, the assembled cabal of editors was given a tour of the modern internet office. They were agog at the fact that every employee had access to his or her own computer and that the work spaces were larger than those enjoyed by most senior editors at *People's Daily*. There were mumblings about the dreadful decadence and extravagance, and a general sucking of teeth at the sight of our staff, most no older than twenty-five, wearing jeans and open-neck shirts – a striking contrast to the stiff collar and tie normally associated with the PD offices.

In an area just outside my office we had set up two computers with monitors to show off the best of the 'worldwide web' and demonstrate what the other 'great' newspapers of the world were doing online. Our link to the outside world was the humble 28k connection – the fastest available in Beijing at the time. The editors-in-chief stood grudgingly in a semicircle in front of the monitors, as my offsider, Laurie Smith, interpreted my glowing endorsement of all things associated with the internet.

Naturally, I was keen to impress the assembled audience with what News Corp was doing on the web and started bringing up pages of some of the company's newspaper websites in Australia. Perhaps getting a little ahead of myself, I began to talk about the commercial potential for newspaper companies online and pointed out that in Australia, News Limited was putting photographs online for viewing and fee-based download at www.newspix.com.au.

Plucking away at the keyboard, I began typing in the required URL but unknowingly left off the '.au' suffix. Unfortunately, the URL 'newspix.com' had at the time been hijacked by a hardcore pornography site. With my back to the screen I had no inclination of what was happening behind me until I noticed two of the slightly more attentive editors squinting furiously through their glasses at the slowly emerging monitor image.

Half-turning to get a glimpse of the source of their intense interest, I could make out what appeared to be a very buxom, very nude blonde astride an animal of some sort . . . Given the slow speed of our internet connection, the image was loading line by line from the top down (so to speak), giving me time to take considered action and stop the download. I pushed the monitor over so it toppled onto the desk and yanked out the power cord.

'Small technical problem,' I muttered, while reaching over to the keyboard of the other still operating machine. 'Now let's show you what *The New York Times* is up to.'

I went on to preview what others were doing – Time Inc's Path-finder portal, *The Washington Post*, *The Guardian* in London. They were obviously impressed as that day's edition of *The New York Times* came online, and that it was possible to call up individual stories. The editors responded with little more than a few raised eyebrows, some nodding and a lot of shuffling of feet. But I was convinced the blonde bombshell had done us in. Everything they had ever imagined about the evil Murdoch empire had been proven oh so true.

Once the editors filed out after a cursory thank you, I asked our PD partners, Mr Zhang and Mr Gu, if there had been any comments or feedback. They said there was nothing, but a meeting was planned back at the PD compound.

A week later, the irrepressible Mr Zhang, my nominal Deputy General Manager, came into my office and pulled up a chair in front of my desk.

'I think it would be a good idea if we help PD,' he said. 'They want to experiment with an online edition of the *People's Daily*'.

'Help?' I said. 'What do you mean by help?'

'Well, maybe we could give them one of our systems engi-neers – maybe Dr Li,' he said, referring to our most senior engineer. 'And maybe one of our graphics people . . . and maybe they need to borrow our webmaster.'

'Anything else?' I prompted.

'Well, PD doesn't have any money for this so maybe we [as in

News Corp] could lend them [as in 'buy'] a server. No more than a small one – say US$45 000.'

I ran the concept of 'assisting' PD with its online efforts past Rupert and he wholeheartedly agreed. I just never told him we were paying for all of the development, and we somehow managed to hide it in the books.

The *People's Daily* site went live on 1 January 1997, just two weeks before we launched the joint venture ChinaByte site. It was explained to us that it would be 'good manners', not to mention good politics, to allow our partners to go first. This meant the *People's Daily* site was the first Communist Party-controlled media site in China and its launch caused a ripple of excitement throughout the internet community. It was seen as an official imprimatur that 'the internet was OK'. The internet revolution in China had begun in earnest.

We were told that prior to launch the PD hierarchy had arranged a private demonstration of the new PD website for the leaders at Zhongnanhai and also with the ambassadors in London and New York to attest to the fact they could view the site live from afar. Apparently, even the normally unbending hardliner Ding Guangen was forced to admit that one of the virtues of the internet was that it would allow China to project its voice to the world unfettered and uncensored by the politically correct Western media outlets. For their efforts, the comrade editors-in-chief were hailed later that year by the Chinese leadership for their far-sightedness and leading role in the modernisation of the Chinese media, and held up as heroes and role models for their colleagues. And the *People's Daily* website – supported by advertising and apparently profitable – is now available in English, French, Spanish, Russian and Arabic, as well as Chinese.

In the Western media at the time, Murdoch and News Corp were naturally vilified for having been seen to aid and abet *People's Daily* in its internet ambitions. The *Salon* website ran a widely picked-up condemnation of the relationship, which said in part:

> On one side, there's the arch-conservative Murdoch, eager to cut deals with dictators of any ideology in pursuit of a global media monopoly. On the other, there's the *People's Daily*, the mouthpiece of the Chinese Communist Party, probably the most ruthless and successful cabal of killers in power today. As they joke in China: 'The only thing you can trust about the *People's Daily* is the date.'

Perhaps – but in 1997 there were only an estimated one million internet users across the whole of China. Ten years later the numbers are in excess of 120 million. Rupert Murdoch's support for the *People's Daily* internet adventure may have been for other than altruistic reasons. But few would have had either the courage or the temerity to partner with China's Communist

Party mouthpiece and wear the flak.

The fact is, in supporting PD, Rupert caused the Chinese leadership to blink. The shutters were up and the internet altered China irrevocably and forever. And no matter how hard they try, Chinese hardliners will never, ever succeed in getting the shutters down again – not completely, anyway.

8

The Devil's Disciple

The BBC news television crew was ready to roll. I had agreed to an interview because the correspondent had told me she was doing a story on the internet in China and, given my role as the head of one of the country's first joint venture websites, she was keen to record my insights. I sat down at my desk, adjusted my tie and straightened my jacket. She cued the camera and moved the microphone under my chin.

'How does it feel to be the devil's disciple in China?' she asked.

Flummoxed by an ambush question right at the top of the interview I managed a none-too-coherent response about my role in China not being really that at all.

In truth, in 1997 I had two roles. I was the Managing Director of the Chinese joint venture internet company ChinaByte, but my News Corporation business card also announced me as 'Vice

President – China' and, indeed, I was the only company executive resident in China. I was the point of contact in all our negotiations and discussions with the Chinese authorities and I had a direct line of report to Murdoch himself, while constantly ticktacking with STAR TV's Gary Davey in Hong Kong to ensure we were, at the very least, in step.

'What is Murdoch's strategy in China, besides appeasement?' the correspondent quipped next.

Good question – although I declined to answer, firstly on the grounds that I didn't think News Corp needed to share its plans in China with the worldwide audience of the BBC, and secondly because I wasn't sure we actually had a cohesive strategy to discuss if we had wanted to. Ironically, just two weeks before the interview took place I had had a long discussion with Murdoch at his home in Los Angeles on that very issue.

One pleasant Sunday afternoon, seated on the patio of Murdoch's Spanish-style stucco mansion on a hilltop overlooking Beverly Hills, with its sweeping views out to the Pacific and Catalina Island, I was holding forth on why we needed to adopt a strategy that would allow News Corp to negotiate from a position of strength, not one that saw us cravenly seeking the blessing of the Beijing leadership.

'If you bend over and drop your trousers in Beijing, the Chinese are certainly going to take full advantage of the situation,' I expounded. 'But they won't respect you in the morning.'

Murdoch nodded in agreement, but I was not sure he was all that comfortable with the analogy.

'We don't need to be seen kowtowing to the Chinese or apologising for past mistakes, because they will see it as a sign of weakness and move to exploit it. We have technology and the Chinese need technology – by working alongside them in a cooperative manner we can prove we are a trusted partner. Only then is Beijing likely to lift the ban on the STAR TV satellite broadcasts,' I argued.

'Our strategy needs to be one of convincing them that it would be far better to have Rupert Murdoch inside the tent pissing out, than outside the tent pissing in.'

The catalyst for all this was the fact that the Chinese had announced President Jiang Zemin would be making a historic visit to the United States later in 1997. Our nemesis, Ding Guangen, was charged with ensuring, as far as possible, that media coverage of Jiang's first major diplomatic outing was favourable and positive.

'We really do need to convince them that you are the world's most powerful media magnate, and that it is better to have Rupert Murdoch as a friend than an enemy,' I explained.

And to some extent I had already started down that path. The State Council Information Office (SCIO) was forever asking for an updated list of Murdoch's media assets around the world. It would assiduously compile these lists but would often take the liberty of including assets formerly owned but now disposed of – for example, Murdoch's chain of regional newspapers across the US – or exaggerating the circulation, readership and influence of News Corp's Australian dailies. A typographic error might have suggested that the Fox News Channel, which had launched in October 1996 to some 17 million subscribers, might in fact have been reaching 170 million Americans. I don't believe News Corp took the liberty to correct any misapprehension the SCIO might have had in that regard.

However, in no discussion with the SCIO, its masters at the Propaganda Department, or any other member of the Chinese leadership, did I ever offer the prospect of 'favourable or positive' coverage in the News Corp media. And, to their credit, the Chinese never once raised the issue. The only thing I committed to, with Murdoch's consent, was that we would try to ensure 'fair and balanced' reporting of China affairs in all News Corp media outlets and that we would promote a better understanding of China to the outside world.

Part of the SCIO's role was to monitor the way in which the world's media reported and commented on China. When I turned up to our regular meetings with Minister Zeng Jianhui at the SCIO office, he would often open an enormous folder of cuttings with attached translations of reports, commentaries and editorials taken from the Murdoch press. Sometimes he would point out a particular article which he felt was either unbalanced or had failed to report the Chinese viewpoint. He never asked for redress, just made the point that his office was monitoring every scintilla of China coverage in the News Corp media.

Minister Zeng only ever raised two editorial bugbears with me. The first was the BBC, which he detested because he believed its reports from China were almost always 'biased and negative' and hurting China's reputation in Europe. The second was the 'irksome Mr Jonathan Mirsky', then East Asia Editor of the Murdoch-owned London *Times*.

Regarding the BBC, Zeng had a willing ally in Murdoch, who had long believed it to be an unwelcome, publicly subsidised competitor to his own broadcasting ambitions in the UK. He had taken the decision to drop the BBC from the STAR TV satellite bouquet in 1994 without hesitation and despite the enormous storm of criticism he knew would be directed at him for the move. There was, of course, little he could do in the UK to change the BBC's editorial stance on China. We could, however, offer an alternative.

I suggested to Murdoch that Sky News should open a bureau in Beijing to provide a 'fair and balanced' alternative to the perceived bias of the BBC. I knew the SCIO would fast-track the approval of a news bureau because it would be in its interests to have another voice reporting China to the UK and Europe. Murdoch agreed to talk with the Sky News management. Within six months, Sky News had appointed veteran foreign correspondent James Furlong to Beijing. Furlong had distinguished himself as a correspondent covering the African conflict before ending up back in London. Aware of his proprietor's commercial interests in China, he came to see me soon after taking up residence in Beijing in late 1998.

Interestingly, Murdoch had put no caveats on the operations of the new Sky News bureau. I repeated to Furlong what Murdoch had confided to me – that any reporting should be balanced, and if Sky was going to be critical of China it should allow the Beijing leadership the opportunity to give its side of the story. Murdoch had actually been concerned about not doing anything that might compromise the Sky News service as it was increasingly taking market share from the BBC in the UK and he wanted to protect its reputation.

'As far as I know,' I told Furlong, 'the only thing the boss had indicated was that Sky News should try to cover some of the positive aspects of China's economic development; the rising living standards, improved services and its opening up to the world. Apart from that, nothing is off limits.' His first story was on the dissident Wei Jingsheng's apparent ill-treatment by the Chinese government.

After a near three-year stint in Beijing, Furlong returned to London where he served as Sky News' Defence and Royal Correspondent. In October 2003, then aged forty-four, he took his own life after having been unceremoniously abandoned by the Sky News management over allegations that during the first Iraq war he had failed to identify as file footage some video of a cruise missile being fired from a British submarine. The allegations were a minor blemish on an otherwise distinguished career.

The matter of the London *Times* was a rather more delicate issue. *The Times* had had a very long association with China, going back to 1896 when it had employed the Australian-born adventurer and journalist G E Morrison as its Peking correspondent. Through his lucid accounts of life in China, particularly the siege of the foreign legations by the Righteous and Harmonious Fists – the Boxers – in 1900, the young writer become known to newspaper readers throughout the English-speaking world as 'Morrison of Peking'. One hundred years later, the Beijing leadership were still of the view that *The Times* was one of the great and most influential newspapers of the world (along with *People's Daily*, in their view). Unfortunately, the warmth with which they had once regarded its correspondent Morrison for his honest portrayals of life from the point of view of the ordinary Chinese did not carry over to one of his later successors, Jonathan Mirsky.

In the lead-up to the events of 1989, Mirsky, a long-time China-watcher and academic, was China correspondent of the London *Observer* newspaper. Like so many of his peers, his reporting of the time was buoyed with an enthusiasm for the pace of economic reform and apparent liberalisation that was sweeping the nation under the relatively open-minded leadership of Hu Yaobang and Zhao Ziyang. But Mirsky was also a courageous witness to the student demonstrations in Tiananmen Square outside the front gates of the Forbidden City, from mid-April to June. The students were demanding an end to official corruption, a free press and the departure of the country's two widely despised leaders, Xiaoping and Premier Li Peng.

Mirsky was in Tiananmen Square in the early hours of 4 June, when the People's Army tanks rolled in and over the demonstrators. He watched as the soldiers beat unarmed people to the ground and shot them where they lay. Mirsky did not escape unscathed, being beaten by the security forces as they cleared any and everyone from the square – they knocked out two of his teeth and broke his left arm. He could never forget or forgive Deng Xiaoping and the ageing revolutionaries who had ordered the bloody massacre of some 400 unarmed students and civilians in the name of restoring order. Understandably, in the months and years after Tiananmen, Mirsky railed and ranted against the excesses of the Beijing leadership – the human rights abuses and the persecution of the dissident students – and wrote in support of the families of the victims. He became such a thorn in the side of the Chinese that in 1991 the SCIO had his visa revoked, effectively banning him from China.

In 1993 Mirsky was employed by *The Times* as its East Asia Editor, based in Hong Kong where he would continue to write his damning critiques of the Chinese leadership. He was increasingly a lone voice as new correspondents arrived in China, many of them more interested in the financial boom and the massive explosion in wealth that was occurring on China's eastern seaboard than they were with the fate of the former student protesters or of perceived human rights abuses.

The SCIO was perplexed that Murdoch, who on the one

hand professed his friendship for China, would on the other hand allow *The Times* to continue to publish Mirsky's outpourings from Hong Kong.

'The Chinese have a problem with *The Times* and Jonathan Mirsky's commentaries on China,' I told Murdoch, as we sat outside on the patio, overlooking the sprawling mansions of Beverly Hills. 'Mirsky drives the Chinese crazy with his reporting on the fate of dissidents, human rights, Tibet . . . and they struggle to see how or why you can't do anything about it.'

Murdoch groaned.

'There is nothing I could do if I wanted,' he said. 'The British Parliament has virtually passed legislation demanding I guarantee the independence of *The Times*. No, no . . . if I moved to do something about Mirsky they would be all over me. Leave it – leave it with me.'

In May 1997, Peter Stothard, then editor of *The Times*, made a ten-day trip to China as a guest of *People's Daily*. As part of News Corporation's role in promoting 'mutual understanding' of China to the world and the world to China, I had engineered a 'sister relationship' between the two newspaper organisations. Late the previous year, the president of *People's Daily*, Shao Huaze, had visited the United Kingdom, ostensibly as a guest of *The Times*, although orchestrated through Murdoch's office in London. The all-expenses-paid visit had included a week at the Ritz Hotel, a weekend at a deer-hunting lodge in Scotland, a private tour of the British Museum and drinks with the Prime Minister, John Major.

People's Daily was now reciprocating the 'hospitality' and Stothard was being hosted in China by his counterparts, although a promised interview with President Jiang Zemin had been cancelled. An audience with Vice Premier Zhu Rongji was proffered in its place – an event that very nearly scuttled our entire diplomatic offensive to date.

Both the *Times* editor and I were under the impression that the meeting with China's effervescent financial czar was an interview opportunity. Zhu, himself, believed Stothard was making a courtesy call. So when Stothard produced his notebook and asked a tough question about the fate of political dissidents in China, we very nearly had a political disaster on our hands.

'What are you asking?' snapped back a clearly very indignant Zhu. 'That is not the way to hold a discussion between friends.' He made as if ready to walk out.

Turning his back on Stothard, Zhu began a heated discussion with the group of advisers and apparatchiks by his side. An equally dismayed Stothard turned to me and our *People's Daily* minders to see what he had done to offend. There were worried looks all round the room. Eventually, after some discussion, it was explained that *People's Daily* had not requested an interview with the Deputy Premier but an opportunity for Stothard to a have an 'informal chat' with the Chinese leader, the same as had taken place between Shao and John Major. Stothard put away the notebook and apologised for the misunderstanding, Zhu nodded and proceeded to expand on a whole range of topics, from Tibet and Tiananmen to the extraordinary challenges he faced on a day-to-day basis trying to juggle the competing concerns of the nation's economic transformation. Zhu was engaging, insightful and relatively open in his discussions and made a significant impression on Stothard.

Mirsky would later claim that Stothard had humiliated himself in front of the Deputy Premier by apologising for asking about political dissidents. It was not true. However, the meeting with Zhu, and Stothard's subsequent meetings with a range of Chinese officials, British diplomats and businessmen, as well as his firsthand view of the transformation and modernisation of China, did raise doubts about the pertinence of Mirsky's writings from his banished position in Hong Kong.

In the months following Stothard's return to London, far fewer articles by his East Asia Editor appeared in print, to the point that Mirsky formally complained, inquiring as to why '90 per cent of his articles on China were being spiked'. Mirsky retired from the position in November 1997 and returned to London, where *The Times* surprisingly offered him a retainer as a 'China Writer' although few of his submissions were ever published. He quit *The Times* altogether in disgust in March 1998, citing the 'heavy hand' of Murdoch all over the paper.

It is doubtful Murdoch ever issued *The Times*' editor an edict to deal with Mirsky – certainly not in any direct sense. Stothard had a reputation for dogged independence and would have likely rebelled if pushed in that direction. More likely, after his trip to China, Stothard believed that for his readers the story had moved beyond Tiananmen and the democracy movement, to the economic miracle that was turning China on its head and creating a new superpower.

It was no matter that the reality had been that Mirsky had resigned in his own right and of his own accord. In our long march to rehabilitation in China, it was another offering we could make to our masters in Beijing – a head on a platter, and one gratefully received.

In terms of my strategy discussion with Murdoch, there was one more item on my agenda. It was the issue of the Whitehall Palace speech and how we would deal with it.

'The speech still really rankles with the Chinese,' I told him, 'especially Li Peng, who apparently took it all very personally. He was the one who actually instituted the ban on satellite dishes across the country.

'We need to get something on the public record. We can't retract what you said, but we might be able to put the remarks in context, explain that you were talking about the unfolding events in Eastern Europe at the time, and outline a more acceptable philosophy for the company's views on investing in China.'

Murdoch pondered for a bit, then said he had agreed to give a keynote address to the International Federation of the Periodical Press (FIPP) World Publishers' Conference in Tokyo later in May. I offered to write the speech and Murdoch granted me the use of his wife Anna's office, next to his on the Twentieth Century Fox lot. It might have been better had he told the security people at Fox as well. The following day when I accidentally tripped the 'panic button' surreptitiously hidden under the tabletop of Anna's work desk, I suddenly found myself confronted by a phalanx of armed guards. Instead of the blonde Mrs Murdoch, they had found a bald, bearded man sitting in her place. There was some explaining to do while I kept my hands very, very still on the desk.

When the speech was delivered in Tokyo on 15 May 1997, it was widely picked up by the international media. It contained a brief *mea culpa*: 'China has proved the sceptics, including myself, wrong, by not shunning new information technologies, but embracing them.'

But there was only one paragraph in the speech that really mattered: 'Advances in telecommunications contribute to the "universalisation" of cultural interests and lifestyles. However, nations retain their own social and moral values that the media must take into account. China is a distinctive market with distinctive social and moral values that Western companies must learn to abide by.'

Murdoch was putting it on the record that despite the inferences made in the Whitehall Palace speech about the liberating aspects of satellite technology, as far as China was concerned he was agreeing to play by the rules – China's rules.

Back in Beijing, every relevant Chinese government official received a copy of the Murdoch speech as well as extracts from the world's press coverage. It must have been well received. In early June, Murdoch received an official invitation to be a VIP guest at the July handover of Hong Kong to Chinese authority, and an offer to be an adviser to the former colony's new Chief Executive, Tung Chee Hwa. It was a small step – but a step in the right direction.

9

Vicissitudes

At the stroke of midnight, 1 July 1997, China's President Jiang Zemin gripped the podium centre stage at the Hong Kong Convention Centre to declare that China had resumed sovereignty over Hong Kong, ending 156 years of British colonial rule.

British soldiers then lowered the Union Jack for the last time to the strains of 'God Save the Queen', as China's Red Star banner was hoisted in its place alongside the new flag of Hong Kong.

'The return of Hong Kong to the motherland after a century of vicissitudes indicates that from now on our Hong Kong compatriots have become true masters of this Chinese land, and that Hong Kong has now entered a new era of development,' intoned the President, in Mandarin.

In the audience, one billionaire media magnate decided he'd had enough. As his fellow guests jostled for position by the Convention Centre's elaborate glass windows to get a view of the world's most expensive ever fireworks display exploding over the Hong Kong Harbour, Rupert Murdoch saw his chance for a discreet exit in the opposite direction.

Murdoch had been quite chuffed to learn he was on the official VIP guest list for the Hong Kong handover ceremony – although somewhat disconcerted on arrival to learn that the list ran to some 4000 names. Nevertheless, it was a sign of a warming in the previously frosty relationship with Hong Kong and one that was seemingly confirmed by a separate invitation to act as a Special Adviser to Beijing's first handpicked Hong Kong Chief Executive, Tung Chee Hwa.

In the two days prior to the official handover Murdoch had met with the new head of China's Ministry of Foreign Affairs Office in Hong Kong, Ma Yuzhen, the urbane former Ambassador to Great Britain, whom he had gotten to know in friendlier times prior to the 1993 Whitehall Palace speech. He was received warmly by Ma, who would be Beijing's 'man in Hong Kong' after the handover.

But the ceremony itself was a bore for Murdoch. Nearly four hours of long-winded speeches, delivered first in Mandarin and then translated into English, were making for a very long evening for someone who could barely sit still for a few minutes, let alone be parted from a phone for any length of time whatsoever. The first part of the evening concluded, Murdoch decided to make a dash for it.

So even as Britain's Prince Charles and former colonial governor

Chris Patten were being driven from the handover ceremony to
the harbour front in pouring rain, where the royal yacht *Britannia*
waited to bear them away from Hong Kong, Murdoch, who had
managed to hail a cab, was hurtling back through the harbour tun-
nel to Kowloon and the sanctuary of his room at the plush Regent
Hotel. Or so he thought.

The handover celebrations were marred by atrociously wet and
humid conditions which saw the last governor drenched to the bone
as he took the final salute, watched by a troop of VIPs huddled under
dripping umbrellas. The entire waterfront area around Kowloon,
including several blocks in the vicinity of the Regent Hotel, had been
cordoned off to allow hundreds of thousands of Hong Kong locals to
get to the harbour to watch the spectacular fireworks display, paid for
by some of the former colony's wealthiest tycoons, eager to impress
the visiting Beijing dignitaries with their largesse.

Murdoch was forced to bail out of his cab several blocks from
the hotel and make his way on foot through the labyrinth of small
streets and alleys that make up the Tsim Sha Tsui shopping area.
He became hopelessly lost. When it was not showering rain, the
heat and humidity was intense and energy-sapping. Murdoch had
left behind his mobile phone – since security arrangements at the
entrance to the Convention Centre precluded them – and for nearly
two hours he wandered about in circles in the steamy, fetid atmosphere apparently unable to elicit an intelligible response from the
many locals he accosted to ask for directions.

Inside the Regent I was busy partaking of the swankiest party in town – the US$320-a-head all-night soirée which featured a British colonial theme until midnight when it switched to 'Chinese Imperial Court'. Somewhere between glasses of champagne at around 2.30 a.m. one of my colleagues brought to my attention a hotel bellboy parading about the downstairs lobby area carrying a message board with my name and room number on it. Making myself known to the bellboy, I was escorted to the concierge desk.

'I am sorry to disturb you, Mr Dover, but there is a gentleman at the car park security gate who is demanding entry to the hotel. He has no ticket to the party, no room key and appears to be carrying no identification. He has asked that you might go down and vouch for him,' the concierge whispered discreetly in my ear, as if to avoid any hint of controversy that might upset the well-heeled hotel guests.

Escorted by two hotel security staff, in the event that there might be any trouble with the would-be interloper, I was led down the hotel's front steps to the driveway cordoned off with barricades, which had been erected to check the push of a vast crowd of onlookers who had gathered to get a peek at some of Hong Kong's most famous and glamorous pop stars inside at the hotel party. There, pushed up against the barricade, was one very dishevelled and bedraggled billionaire, who, having finally managed to propel himself through the throng, was now being denied entry to the hotel by the security guards.

Tie discarded, his suit coat hanging over one shoulder, and wet through by a combination of perspiration and rain drizzle, Murdoch was in fact in surprisingly good humour.

'What an adventure,' he blurted. 'Been out there for ages, trying to find my way, walking up one dead end after another. Didn't have a mobile phone and had left my wallet behind. Couldn't seem to make myself understood to the locals when I asked for directions . . . I'd ask three of them where the hotel was and they would all point in different directions.'

I inquired as to whether he was going to join the party. He declined, excused himself and said he would go to his room, take a hot shower and go to bed.

'Big day tomorrow, big day,' he said as he disappeared into the hotel lift.

Indeed, it was already tomorrow and we were set to depart for Beijing for Murdoch's first meeting with a member of the Beijing leadership – Vice Premier Zhu Rongji.

The meeting with Zhu was the first indication that there was division in the ranks of the Chinese Politburo about how to deal with the Murdoch threat. I came to realise that China's Ministry of Foreign Affairs (MFA) had a much more worldly view of Murdoch and how to deal with him. Unlike the ideologically driven Propaganda Department headed by Ding Guangen, the MFA came under the purview of the urbane career diplomat Vice Premier Qian Qichen, concurrently the Minister for Foreign Affairs. Qian's diplomatic duties had provided him with extensive exposure to the West and, more particularly, to the foibles of the Western media. He had met Murdoch briefly a number of times at various official functions in New York, Washington and London and was firmly of the view that China should be reaching out and engaging the media tycoon, rather than antagonising him to the extent he became an enemy and not a friend, especially in the lead-up to the all-important visit of President Jiang Zemin to the US later that year. The MFA's dossiers on the media magnate, filed from its embassies around the world, were all too full of examples of just how quickly Murdoch could switch his political alliances.

Early in May 1997, Vice Premier Zhu had made an official visit to Australia. China's Ambassador to Australia, Hua Jundao, had included a brief meeting with Murdoch in the itinerary, on the basis that he was the Chairman and Chief Executive of News Corporation, then still an Australian-registered company and a very significant player in the nation's media. Murdoch had to pull out of the meeting at the last minute as he was detained in the US on a deal he thought would deliver him his other prized acquisition – the US satellite television operator DIRECTV (although it fell through and it would be another eight years before he finally won control of the platform).

Soon after, I was contacted in Beijing by an official from the MFA. She suggested that should Murdoch write directly to Vice Premier Zhu through the Chinese Embassy in Canberra, a request for a meeting might be favourably received. Up until this point requests for Murdoch to meet even officials of ministerial rank were being politely fobbed off. Furthermore, she hinted that it would be best that any proposed visit to Beijing by Murdoch be 'in a private capacity' so as not to alert 'official channels', which I took to mean the Propaganda Department and the SCIO.

On 26 May, I drafted a letter for Murdoch which we had delivered to Ambassador Hua at the Chinese Embassy in Canberra. Two days later, we received a signed letter back from Vice Premier Zhu indicating that he had received Murdoch's missive 'with pleasure'.

'I hope that you could make another visit to China soon and believe that there would be an opportunity for us to meet in the future,' Zhu wrote.

We immediately responded by saying that 'by chance' Murdoch was intending to make a 'private visit' to Beijing just after the Hong Kong handover, his first in two years since his effective freezing out by the Chinese authorities. Zhu responded that the timing was suitable and that arrangements would be handled by the MFA.

The meeting was to take place at Zhongnanhai, the sprawling villa-like complex of gardens, meeting rooms, underground tunnels and official residences adjacent to the Forbidden City, where many of the Communist Party's highest leaders lived and worked.

When we arrived at the ornate meeting room that had once housed some of China's imperial mandarins, the Vice Premier was already seated on a large throne-like wooden chair. He motioned for Murdoch to take a seat on a similar chair beside him. Zhu had clearly been leafing through a large file placed on a table beside him that bore Murdoch's name on the front cover. Zhu had a formidable reputation as a tough, hands-on manager, intolerant of flunkeyism and corruption but with a self-deprecating sense of humour and directness that endeared him to the international community.

An extremely well-briefed Zhu began by asking his visitor to recount how he had built his empire from its humble beginnings in Adelaide to be one of the world's great media companies. As Murdoch gave a modest account of his rise to power, a genuinely intrigued Zhu would frequently interrupt and ask him to elaborate on certain points, and to expand on some of the challenges he had faced.

After some minutes, Zhu leant across, put his hand on Murdoch's wrist and looked him in the eye.

'I see when you needed to expand your business interests in the United States, you decided to become a US citizen,' Zhu said in Mandarin. 'Maybe you should think of applying for Chinese citizenship to further your business interests in China.'

As the Vice Premier's words were translated into English, Murdoch visibly reeled back, blinked and started to splutter a reply, not knowing quite what to make of the proposition.

Zhu burst into laughter, adding in perfect English himself: 'Just joking, just joking!' Murdoch relaxed and joined in the joke – which was either just that or a very perceptive dig by Zhu at what he saw as Murdoch's absolute pragmatism when it came to doing business.

Zhu and Murdoch prattled on for more than an hour, covering a range of topics that touched on the world economy, education and the challenges of China's opening up, modernisation and reform. The media magnate was particularly encouraged to hear the Vice Premier indicate that the nation's information technology sector would also soon be opened up to reform, thus waving the carrot of News Corporation participating in China's ongoing development.

Murdoch left after the meeting aboard a commercial flight to London, extremely pleased with what had very clearly been a warm, open and honest discussion with Zhu. He believed it was a sign that his efforts to date had been acknowledged and things were on the improve. He also kept his sense of humour. The following week he wrote back to Zhu, thanking him for taking the time to meet with him: 'I think it may be a little premature to take up your suggestion of applying for Chinese citizenship to further my business interests in China – well, at least for the time being!' Murdoch, even tongue-in-cheek, was keeping his options open.

The following week, I again heard from my contact inside the Chinese MFA, who indicated the Ministry had also been pleased with the outcome of the meeting. However, she added that the Ministry believed there was another hurdle that Murdoch needed to get over – the outstanding issue of his Whitehall Palace speech.

She said this still remained an issue at the highest levels of the Chinese leadership and that it was the Ministry's view that perhaps a personal letter from Murdoch addressed to President Jiang Zemin and Premier Li Peng which put the speech in 'context' might be in order.

After discussion with Murdoch, a letter was drafted and passed through the MFA for delivery to the Chinese leaders. In it Murdoch said he was 'alarmed to hear the comments I had made in the 1993 speech about the impact of satellite technologies on the unfolding political events in Europe at the time, had been construed to suggest I was referring to China and the Chinese leadership'.

'This was never the case. I apologise for any misunderstanding this may have caused. I remain firmly committed to China and the development of the Chinese economy.'

Importantly, Murdoch again made no offers of positive coverage of the affairs in China other than to note that he had 'tried to ensure that [his] company's newspaper and television operations provide balanced, fair and objective coverage of events in China'.

'I regret any misunderstandings that may have occurred in the past in relation to my or my company's view on China. I can assure you that I remain a good friend of China, committed to its taking its rightful place on the world stage and willing to participate in its economic development and growth.'

Later I heard from my contacts inside China's foreign ministry that Ding Guangen had been incensed when he had heard of the meeting between Zhu Rongji and Murdoch, given that it had circumvented the strategic roadmap previously put in place to monitor the media proprietor's every move inside China. A fierce debate apparently took place about the pace at which Murdoch's rehabilitation should proceed.

Qian Qichen pushed the foreign ministry's line that with President Jiang Zemin's groundbreaking visit to the US scheduled for late October, it would be counterproductive to alienate the world's most powerful media magnate. Jiang would be the first Chinese leader to visit the US since 1985 and both sides were hoping the Sino-American summit would help remove at least some of the contentious elements in the relationship. The Chinese attached enormous prestige to the visit and were intent on ensuring the international media coverage surrounding it was favourable.

It seemed that Qian's argument prevailed. In August I received word that a request by Murdoch to make an 'official' visit to China in mid-October would be well received, coming as it would just prior to President Jiang's scheduled departure for the US summit. Murdoch readily agreed to the proposal and was even hopeful that the visit might realise the opportunity for him to have an audience with the Chinese President himself. I did my best to dampen the boss's enthusiasm in this regard but Murdoch was becoming impatient with the pace of progress and beginning to think that his commercial rivals were in position to gain some advantage over him in the market – despite all he had done to appease the Chinese authorities.

Murdoch had absolute faith in his own ability to sit down with the world's political leaders and reach some accommodation which would serve their mutual interests. He had proved that time and time again in the markets in which he operated – the UK, Australia and the US.

'When do you think I can meet with President Jiang?' he would regularly ask. 'If I can just sit down and talk with Jiang, I'm sure we can work something out. We just need to get a meeting so we can sort this all out. When do you think we can arrange it?'

10

Absolution

Protocol would probably require one to be on time for a meeting with one's nemesis. So it was that Rupert Murdoch and his entourage of News Corp executives had arrived early at Beijing's Great Hall of the People on the morning of 24 October 1997 for a scheduled appointment with Ding Guangen, the head of the Propaganda Department. Our repeated requests for a meeting with President Jiang Zemin had come to naught. But from out of the blue a tantalising invitation had come – to have a meeting with the man who had been instrumental in placing the shackles on Murdoch's media ambitions in China.

This was to be an event carefully stage-managed by Ding and his cohorts. The Propaganda chief was intent on sending a message that he, and he alone, would decide on the pace of Murdoch's rehabilitation in China, and we were to stop trying to circumvent his authority. Any meeting with President Jiang Zemin would be at his timing – and such a time had not arrived. Now, in a clearly symbolic gesture of his power, he insisted that the venue for meeting Murdoch would not be his own office at the Propaganda Department, nor at the SCIO, but one of the ornate meeting rooms of the most imposing building on Tiananmen Square.

The Great Hall of the People is one of the world's architectural marvels, a building so immense that it comprises some 300 meeting rooms, lounges and offices and has a seating capacity of just over 10 000. Its main entrance fronts onto Tiananmen Square and features twelve 25-metre-high grey marble columns topped by an enormous lintel bearing the national emblem. As we waited outside for our summons, Murdoch stood by one of the towering columns amiably chatting with Wendi Deng, who had first accompanied us as interpreter and guide during a visit to Shanghai two days previously, and who early that morning had taken Murdoch to the Xiushui Market where the tycoon had got his great deal on silk ties. I interrupted their conversation briefly to point out to Murdoch the irony in the timing of the meeting – almost four years to the day since the Chinese had issued a total ban on satellite dishes across the country and declared the News Corporation proprietor *persona non grata*.

We had been summoned to the Great Hall for a meeting with Comrade Ding, who up until that time had been the faceless puppet-master to whom all our Chinese media contacts had deferred in the most reverential of manners. A member of the Politburo, he was one of its most secretive yet powerful figures holding sway across the entire cultural landscape of China.

His department vetted every book, every manuscript, every screenplay that touched on the Party, its leaders, political or social issues, or policies relating to foreign diplomacy, nationalities or religion. It issued edicts informing publishers and editors which stories could be covered and how they should be reported. Ding was widely despised by many in the media for his hard-line approach in curtailing any attempts to push the defined limits of what might pass for freedom of expression. Most importantly, he was in charge of preventing the spread of 'spiritual pollution' which allowed 'anti-socialist values to creep into Chinese culture'. And to that end, he was in charge of Rupert Murdoch.

At the appointed hour, one of Ding's minions appeared at the entrance and beckoned for us to follow him down a long corridor past seemingly endless meeting rooms, each named after a different province in China and decorated after the local style of its namesake, until we came to the Liaoning Hall. As we entered, a tallish Chinese figure, with a broad comb-over and a pair of the large rimmed spectacles favoured by President Jiang, rose from his chair and walked over to greet Murdoch with an outstretched hand.

'Good morning, Mr Murdoch,' he said. 'My name is Ding Guangen and I am pleased to meet you.'

Ding indicated that Murdoch and his entourage – which included me, my deputy and our interpreter Laurie Smith and Wendi Deng – be seated. To our astonishment, sitting directly across from us was the head of every major Chinese media department: Zeng Jianhui (Minister of the State Council Information Office [SCIO]), Sun Jiazheng (Minister for Radio, Film and Television), Yang Weiguang (President of CCTV), Shao Huaze (President of *People's Daily*), and Li Bing, the senior SCIO cadre assigned by Ding to cover our every move in China. It was an impressive show of power by Ding, who wanted it to be made very clear that all these ministers reported to him.

'Well, Mr Murdoch,' began Ding, 'I understand your company News Corporation is an Australian company. Tell me, what does it do?'

Murdoch blinked. He wasn't sure if this was an attempted put-down or a genuine inquiry, given Ding was probably better briefed than most on the operations of the company. Nevertheless, he began a long recital of the various businesses under the News Corp umbrella, reeling off the various Australian, British and US holdings. Ding listened attentively, nodding his head knowingly until Murdoch touched on Twentieth Century Fox.

Ding suddenly became very animated, leant forward in his chair and started to gush enthusiastically about the great classic movies from the Fox studios.

'Oh, I am a great admirer of the films of Twentieth Century Fox,' he said. 'You know, we have a very large collection of Hollywood classic films at Zhongnanhai and I enjoy watching them very much . . . Oh, Tyrone Power – such a great actor,' he said.

Murdoch was momentarily stunned by the sudden change in direction the discussion had taken but managed to blurt out something about 'bringing some copies of the Tyrone Power films for Minister Ding next time he came to Beijing'. The Propaganda Department head nodded approvingly.

Murdoch continued his spiel: 'News Corporation is very keen to explore opportunities for cooperation in China, based of course on respect and understanding of China's unique cultural and social values. Of course, my company has much to learn about doing business in China and we have made some mistakes—'

Ding raised his hand, indicating Murdoch should stop.

'The issues of the past should be laid to rest and we should make a fresh start,' Ding announced.

Then pointing to his assembled ministers, he went on: 'For the future, here are the people who manage the media businesses in China – all your future dealings should be through them.'

It was absolution. Murdoch had been forgiven for his past misdemeanours. He was off the blacklist.

'News Corporation and the relevant departments in China should look to the future and seek to build a positive and constructive relationship,' added Ding.

We would later discover just what the Chinese had in mind by a 'positive and constructive relationship'.

Minister Zeng then chipped in to remind us of the importance of President Jiang's visit to the US the following week, reiterating the need for the international media to ensure that its coverage of controversial issues relating to China 'reflected all sides of the issues in an accurate and objective manner'. He then produced a pile of videotapes of what he termed 'background to issues pertinent to President Jiang's visit' and asked that we pass them on to the News Corporation broadcasting outlets in the US and Europe. Murdoch agreed that we would gratefully pass on the material, which was largely footage of Jiang meeting a variety of world leaders and obviously compiled to show off his statesman-like qualities on the world stage. (And, indeed, it did prove useful for the Fox News network, which had little archival footage of the Chinese leader in its library.)

Zeng then went on to extol the virtues of the Phoenix Television channel, in particular the way in which it was providing 'balanced and positive' coverage of events in China. There was something ingenuous about Zeng's tone in all of this and only later did we begin to suspect just how much of a vested interest the SCIO had in the operation of the joint venture channel. We had known Phoenix Chief Executive Liu Changle had good relations with the SCIO, but it transpired that Zeng's office had backed the deal all the way to the top as a means of managing Murdoch's entry into China – the SCIO were Liu's political backers.

The meeting broke up with warm smiles and handshakes all round. Murdoch had met his nemesis and emerged not just unscathed, but with a blessing to go forward and 'cooperate'. It was a very significant achievement to be off the blacklist after four years knocking on doors with little chance of being invited in. But the reality was that Murdoch and News Corp were now simply back on the level playing field, having to compete with any number of rivals seeking the same goal – landing rights for their satellite television channels in China.

Positive as the meeting had been, there was still no indication from Comrade Ding that a meeting between Murdoch and President Jiang was even on the table, nor was there even a hint that the ban on satellite dishes would be lifted. Murdoch continued to brood about this. He had by now some US$2 billion invested in the STAR TV operation in Hong Kong and it continued to bleed cash at the rate of around US$2 million a week. He had put another US$40 million in to kick-start the Phoenix joint venture and that too was losing money hand over fist. Murdoch became even more convinced that he needed a one-on-one conversation with Jiang to sort things out. He started to become increasingly agitated and concerned that his rivals – the likes of Time Warner, Hughes Electronics (which owned and operated the rival DIRECTV network in the US) and Viacom – were all out-manoeuvring us on the ground in China. Murdoch was a total believer in 'vertical integration' by which you produced and owned not just the content, but the means to distribute and redistribute it in every territory in which you operated. That a rival satellite operator might hold the key to China forcing Murdoch through its tollgate was a totally unacceptable and unforgivable outcome.

Jiang Zemin's visit to the US was, on the whole, hugely success-ful. Murdoch attended a banquet in Jiang's honour in Los Angeles, but his mood was not helped by the fact he was left off the official White House guest list for the state dinner hosted by President Bill Clinton for his Chinese counterpart – especially as those on the list included Jerry Levin from Time Warner, Frank Biondi from Viacom, Michael Eisner from Disney and the heads of nearly every other major media company in the US.

In November, Murdoch faxed me a copy of an article that had appeared in the international press and asked me to call him imme-diately when I received it. He was extremely agitated at the story's suggestion that Hughes Electronics subsidiary DIRECTV was about to launch a Direct-to-Home (DTH) service in China. Hughes was a competitor in the US and had also launched a rival service to News Corp's JSkyB in Japan. The article quoted the Senior Vice President of Hughes Electronic and President of DIRECTV International, Gareth Chang, suggesting the arrangement with the Chinese authorities was virtually a done deal. Chang was a suave, articulate Chinese-American whom Murdoch had dealt with on a number of occasions in the US. He was now convinced that Chang's Chinese heritage and connections had given Hughes a jump-start in Asia.

In Hong Kong, Gary Davey had received a similar call from Murdoch demanding to know what was going on. We both assured him the story could not be correct. Both of us checked our sources and contacts in China: at the State Administration of Radio, Film and Television (SARFT), which was the regulatory body, and at the SCIO and CCTV. No one knew anything of an impending satellite deal with Hughes, DIRECTV or any other international corporation. Murdoch took us at our word, but sounded less than convinced.

The following week, Murdoch informed me and Davey that he intended to make another visit to Beijing in mid-to late December. We both tried to gently persuade the boss, or 'Old Grumpy' as Davey had taken to calling him, that another visit so soon after his October meeting with Ding might be a bit premature. Murdoch was adamant he was coming – although, as we later learnt, the reasons for doing so were more of a personal nature than strictly business.

Because it was to be an 'official visit' we needed an invitation letter from the SCIO. When I approached Minister Zeng even he groaned with the prospect of another call by Murdoch, but reluctantly agreed. I questioned him about the chances of Murdoch being able to have an audience with President Jiang. He shook his head and said it was 'still too soon, too soon'. It seemed that while News Corp was now officially off the blacklist, the Propaganda Department wanted time to see that we played within the rules and could indeed 'work cooperatively and constructively' with the relative Chinese departments. We may have been off the blacklist but we were still on the watch list.

Murdoch was not happy that the prospects of a meeting with Jiang still appeared to be some way off. However, I reminded him that Ding had hinted strongly that 'technology in particular was an area in which News Corporation could make a contribution to China's economic development'. To that end I had introduced News Corp's technology arm News Digital Systems (NDS) to our counterparts at SARFT and they had expressed a good deal of interest in our encryption technology. I told Murdoch we should make a big play of our expertise in that area with the ministers we would meet during the December visit.

By this stage it was becoming clear that while the Chinese leadership viewed television as a crucial means of achieving its propaganda aims, it was never going to allow a foreign satellite broadcaster unfettered access to its backyard. Increasingly, the government was looking to cable to deliver its television services to the people, because cable was more readily controlled from a single distribution point – and it was 'control' that the Chinese authorities demanded. A set-top box that contained a Chinese-derived conditional access system would give it that control. If NDS were able to partner with the Chinese regulator to produce such a system it would deliver enormous royalties, while ensuring News Corp stayed in the box seat compared to its competitors. It turned out to be one of the most profitable moves News Corp would make in China. It was also one of the last good moves I would make there, as I was fast running out of ideas to push our cause forward and Murdoch was running out of patience.

Three weeks later he was again on the phone. He had heard that Jerry Levin from Time Warner, fresh back from China, was proudly expounding to all and sundry about his meeting with President Jiang Zemin in Beijing. It was meant to be a one-hour meeting but the two had got on so well Jiang had asked him to stay for dinner and they had chatted on for nearly four hours.

When I checked with my contacts at China's foreign ministry, it was explained thus:

Mr Levin is a known quantity – Time Warner has no great aspirations to enter the China market in a big way. Mr Murdoch wishes for China to open its doors to his satellite television broadcasts. Mr Levin wishes to host a conference in Shanghai [the Fortune Global Forum] and bring 400 of the world's top business executives to showcase China. Mr Murdoch wants to put advertising in the living room of every household in China.

Some of the leaders still regard Mr Murdoch with great suspicion. It is like having Genghis Khan at the Palace Gates – he may tell you he is your friend, but then he might also rise up and strike at one thousand places . . . You will need to be more patient.

I attempted to explain the situation to Murdoch in somewhat more subtle terms. However, he didn't seem to want to listen. In regard to matters relating to China, it was clear someone else now had his ear.

11

Enter Wendi

Murdoch without a telephone was like an alcoholic without a drink. He would grow agitated, fidgety, desperately looking for a fix. Murdoch ran his empire by phone and at almost any time of his day – every day, 6 a.m. in the gym or midnight in his hotel room – there was an executive he could call somewhere in the world who was in the middle of their day and able to take a call from the boss.

He would phone from his car, the private jet or from home – anywhere he could get a line. Sometimes he would get the time zones wrong and apologise for disturbing you at an odd hour or on vacation. There was usually no greeting, just a precise 'Murdoch here!' Once, when he woke me from a deep slumber in Hanoi at 4 a.m., I had the temerity to respond 'Murdoch who?' There was a long pause at the other end of the line. There was, after all, only one Murdoch.

And he had a phenomenal recall for telephone numbers. He'd punch away with his index finger at a mobile phone keypad while in the back of a limousine in China, calling one of his people in Los Angeles. If he'd missed them in the office, he'd pause and comment, 'I'll try him at home . . . or at the ranch'. *Punch, punch!* 'No luck. I'll try Les at home in London.' *Punch, punch, punch!* And all the time he'd just pluck the numbers from his head.

But if Murdoch expected his executives to be on-call at any given time of their day, so too did he make himself available to take a call. If he were not in the office you could call him at home – be it LA, the ranch in Carmel, London or New York – even if he were on holiday in the South Pacific on his luxury yacht *Morning Glory*, he would take a call by satellite phone.

The latter, he confided to me once, so annoyed his second wife that Anna took to unplugging the satellite phones on the boat and hiding them so he would at least take some time to relax. But, he added, he became so cantankerous she had to put them back.

So it was that in late 1997 those who were in telephone contact with Murdoch at least once a week were more than a little flummoxed when his private secretary of some thirty-four years, Dot Wyndoe, advised that the boss would be unavailable for the next four to five days because he was going on a 'walking tour of Wales'. Murdoch taking leisurely walks in the country was hard to believe; Murdoch without a phone and not contactable was incredible.

By a strange coincidence, the very same week, Wendi Deng,

who had been working with me in Beijing during the previous few months, advised that she had to attend a wedding in New York at short notice and needed some time off – just four or five days. She would take the Thursday night flight to New York but be back at work the following Wednesday morning.

The trips, of course, may have been perfectly innocent, but given the recent train of events, for the first time an inkling that something was developing between our ageing media magnate boss and the 29-year-old Business Development executive started to firm into something like suspicion.

I had introduced Murdoch to Wendi at a cocktail party at Hong Kong's Harbour Plaza Hotel just prior to the 1 July 1997 handover celebrations, attended mainly by STAR TV executives. Because Gary Davey was delayed in India it was left to me to play host.

As an introduction, it was pretty straightforward: 'Murdoch, this is Wendi Deng. Wendi is working with us in Business Development in China.' Wendi was a Yale MBA graduate who had been with STAR TV less than a year. She was tall, attractive, intelligent, vivacious and confident, and immediately had the Chief Executive's full attention.

After the cocktail party, on the way back to the Regent Hotel, where Murdoch always stayed on his visits to Hong Kong, he remarked how 'impressive' he found 'the young Chinese women' present at the function. 'Intelligent and full of enthusiasm . . . they're the people who will change China and make it a superpower to be reckoned with. They should be running the country.'

He went on: 'I've found that as you get older, it's important to surround yourself with young people – full of new ideas, energy and enthusiasm. It rubs off on you, revitalises you.' On reflection, I might have missed the pertinence of this observation at the time, and a similar prescient remark from Wendi just a few weeks before.

At a dinner party, at the home of then London *Times* Beijing correspondent James Pringle, the conversation amongst the gathered women had somehow turned to the subject of eligible bachelors. Wendi had roundly announced that her ideal catch would be 'a richer, older man'. It sounded almost flippant at the time but perhaps those of us present should have paid the remark significantly more attention.

None of us who worked and socialised with Wendi were aware then that she had a past very much removed from that of the single, up-and-coming business executive which she now presented to the world. It was a complete surprise when a *Wall Street Journal* investigative report published some years later revealed that she had in fact already been married to an older, if not richer, man. Her first husband, Jake Cherry, was a middle-aged engineer and a married man when their relationship began. They had met a decade earlier when Jake and his wife Joyce were working in Guangzhou, China. Joyce tutored Wendi in English. After a few months, Joyce departed for the West Coast with her two children while Jake stayed on to complete his work as a construction supervisor. It was Jake who suggested to his wife they sponsor Wendi in the US while she attended college.

In 1988 at age nineteen, Wendi came to California, moved in with the Cherrys – sharing a bedroom with the couple's five-year-old daughter – and began her studies. Soon after, Wendi and Jake began a relationship. When Joyce discovered the two were seeing each other she ordered Wendi out of the house. Jake soon followed and moved into a nearby home with Deng, who had enrolled at California State University (CSU) at Northridge. Jake and Wendi married in February 1990. He was fifty-three years old, Wendi just twenty-one. They were barely together for four months before Wendi moved out to take up with a young American by the name of David Wolfe. Wendi and Jake officially divorced in 1992, four months after Wendi received her Green Card, enabling her to live and work in the US. In any case, having graduated from CSU with flying colours, she was on her way to one of America's most prestigious learning institutions – Yale.

By the time Wendi had finished her Masters of Business Administration, again with impressive results, the relationship with Wolfe had also broken down. Oddly, when Wendi was spending long periods in Beijing for STAR TV, Wolfe was also there, working for an investment consultancy. Neither ever mentioned to colleagues and friends that they even knew each other.

Wendi had turned up in Hong Kong in early 1996 as an intern

at STAR TV, having been introduced to STAR's Chief Operating Officer Bruce Churchill by a mutual friend. Her arrival was a revelation in the company at the time. Despite China being the broadcaster's target market, the entire top echelon of the STAR TV management was made up of Anglo-Saxon expatriates, none of whom spoke Mandarin and few of whom, if any, had ever worked in mainland China. Those few 'Chinese' who were employed in senior positions were either Hong Kong-Chinese or Taiwanese – the products of cultures far different from that of Communist China. Wendi at the very least offered some insight into the vagaries of the mainland Chinese business and cultural ethic. At the end of her internship – and long before she had met Murdoch – the STAR TV executive team had unanimously agreed she should be offered a full-time position in business development.

Wendi was hardworking and eager to learn, but also ambitious and absolutely single-minded in her desire to succeed. There was no doubt she put in the long hours required to excel. She impressed everyone with her energy, good humour and mischievous wit. Wendi had an extraordinary ability to absorb information like a sponge, then process and regurgitate it. She knew what she did know, and knew what she didn't know, and she wasn't afraid to ask questions – asking again and again until she had extracted all the information she needed, often ending such sessions with 'I'm sorry I'm asking so many questions'. Well aware of her charms, she was naturally flirtatious with the mainly male executive coterie around her at STAR, and a good number of them were actively vying for her attention.

Wendi was completely devoid of any sense of self-consciousness, which some of her colleagues could mistake for downright rudeness or brashness, but there was always a touch of innocence to her behaviour that was her saving grace. One notable flaw was that she often spoke too much when she might have done better to listen, or inserted herself into a conversation with a comment that was totally unrelated to the discussion.

Within a few months of starting work she had convinced Gary Davey that she needed a more grandiose title on her business card, in order that she might be taken more seriously by her Chinese counterparts during her forays across the border into China. By mid-1997, she was proudly bearing a card from STAR TV anointing her as Vice President – Business Development. Not bad for someone less than a year out of university and with no previous experience in the media. But she was undoubtedly a fast learner, to the point that I was trying to convince her to give up her Hong Kong role and move full-time to Beijing to support me in the mainland China operations.

And all the time she was very discreet about her past, never mentioning her previous marriage or the relationship with Wolfe. When pressed, Wendi would only recount her time at Yale studying for her MBA and how she had worked closely with China's three-time Olympic gold medallist Li Ning, who was struggling to build a clothing brand in the US market.

Three months after the cocktail party Murdoch was back in Hong Kong, en route to Shanghai. The Chinese authorities had hinted they thought it would be a good idea if the News Corp chief, who regularly expressed his admiration for China and the Chinese, might like to get out and see a bit more of the nation other than just Beijing. Consequently I had arranged a trip to Shanghai, the economic heart of China. We had meetings with some of the biggest and most progressive media players in the city, including Shanghai Television and the Shanghai Media Group. Gary Davey was away in India and our regular interpreter was unavailable so it was agreed that Wendi would accompany us to translate at the meetings.

We flew into Shanghai and checked into the historic Peace Hotel, the 1920s centrepiece of old Shanghai. Murdoch was keen to acquaint himself with the city, so in the early evening we set off to walk along the fabulous riverside Bund and the backblocks of the city. To do so involved crossing the wide boulevard that divides the hotel from the Huangpu riverfront. Rather than wait for the traffic lights, Murdoch made an impetuous dash just as a bus hurtled around the corner with the world's most powerful media mogul directly in its sights. Fortunately the startled driver hit the brakes and there was a screeching of tyres and a blaring of horns as the bus trundled to a halt, metres from a somewhat startled Murdoch. Wendi and I looked at each other in horror – losing the Chief Executive to a bus accident in downtown Shanghai would not be a good look.

Bizarrely, as I recounted to Wendi later, my first thoughts had been 'Oh my God, what if he'd been killed? Who do I call first — the News Corp office, the ambulance or my stockbroker?'

Fortuitously perhaps, my mobile phone rang and I was required to go back to the hotel and re-organise our meeting schedule for the next day. Murdoch and Wendi decided to continue their city tour on their own. Wendi took the boss's arm and guided him across the road. When he returned some hours later Murdoch was absolutely abuzz with excitement. He'd had a fascinating discussion with a street vendor of counterfeit cigarettes (he was on the Philip Morris board at the time), and a haircut at a dubious establishment where Wendi had gone to some lengths to explain that 'Mr Foreigner' did not need to avail himself of the other services offered at the back of the room behind the curtain. Although one of the world's wealthiest men, Murdoch couldn't wait to tell his colleagues back home that he'd just had a haircut for under a dollar — including a massive tip. He was radiating pleasure and excitement, completely taken by the city's energy and vitality — at least that's what I thought had inspired him.

The next morning, I trudged down to the hotel gym at 6 a.m. to find Murdoch and Wendi already there, pumping away on a pair of exercise bicycles. I remember noting then that the two of them had struck up quite a remarkable rapport in a short time. Murdoch was fascinated to be talking very openly with an educated, articulate mainland Chinese woman who was able to give him rare insight into Chinese culture and a totally different perspective on developments taking place in what was the world's fastest-growing economy. Wendi had an impish sense of humour that the boss obviously enjoyed, judging by the laughter coming from their corner of the gymnasium room. Wendi seemed to be genuinely surprised that Murdoch had been intently interested in what she had to say and about her observations of STAR TV's strategy in China. She could be disarmingly direct when she wanted.

Over the following weeks and months, it became apparent to both Gary Davey and me that Murdoch was having an ongoing dialogue with Wendi. Murdoch would sometimes sprout what we called 'Wendi-isms' in our weekly conversations, and Wendi would parrot observations that Murdoch had uttered in our business discussions. While it raised our eyebrows, it wasn't in one sense that unusual. If you were asked to draw an organisational chart of News Corp, it would have Murdoch on top and under him a single straight line to everyone else. Frustrating as it was to his executives, Murdoch would often pick up the phone and call anyone, even lower-ranking staff, soliciting opinions on how the business was going. We'd figured that having been impressed with Wendi, her being able to provide a Chinese perspective on STAR TV's aspirations, he was getting another opinion.

Needless to say, few of us at this time had any inclination that the relationship between Murdoch and Anna – after thirty years of marriage – was in serious trouble and headed for the rocks. I got an inkling once, when in the back of a limousine on the way from Beijing Airport to the hotel Murdoch was having a 'yes dear' conversation with Anna on the mobile phone, rolling his eyes upwards and frowning a lot. After the conversation had finished, he turned and said, 'She wants me to slow down, spend time at home, go to all these silly functions . . . Makes me feel I'm getting to be an old man or something.'

So while the 'walking expedition in Wales' set us all thinking, new events were about to make our jaws hit the floor. At this early stage, we'd realised that the boss had taken a shine to Wendi but it still required an enormous leap of faith to turn it into a romance between a 68-year-old prudish media mogul and a 29-year-old Chinese graduate.

In February 1998 Murdoch had agreed to make another visit to China as part of our ongoing fence-mending and relationship-building strategy with the Beijing hierarchy. For the first time we had been granted audiences with key government ministers who in the past had palmed us off on a potpourri of vice ministers and lower-placed acolytes.

The boss, however, was being strangely reticent about his travel plans. First, Murdoch, who had always stayed at the Regent, wouldn't say where he was staying. No, he didn't want us to make a booking; yes, he'd look after it himself; and no, he wasn't sure which hotel it would be. This was a bit difficult given that I usually flew down from Beijing to travel up with him from Hong Kong, in order to brief him on developments and the various issues we would need to raise with individual ministers.

The Beijing meetings were set for Tuesday through to Friday, so we expected Murdoch – whose schedule was always extremely tight and who never wasted a day anywhere if he could avoid it – to fly in early Monday, as usual. Instead, he announced that he would be arriving the Friday before and spending the weekend in Hong Kong 'catching up on the paperwork'.

Two days before his expected arrival, I managed to convince Dot Wyndoe to divulge that the boss had booked into the Shangri-La Hotel on the other side of the Hong Kong Harbour from the Regent. I decided to book in there as well, as I didn't want to be trekking across town trying to meet up with Murdoch to get him briefed and ready for the trip to Beijing. I checked in early on the Friday and, as was the custom, gave my corporate credit card to cover the costs of both the Chief Executive's and my hotel stays. The hotel manager was very excited by the prospect of the great Mr Murdoch gracing the hotel with his presence and set about introducing me to the key hotel staff who would be ensuring Mr Murdoch had a 'memorable' stay.

Just before 6 p.m. Davey and I left for the airport to pick up Murdoch and deliver him to the hotel. As usual, he was travelling unaccompanied and with just his carry-on suit bag and an over-sized briefcase stuffed full of documents and faxes from his operations around the world, in addition to the 'blue folder'. The 'blue folder' was one of Murdoch's concessions to his near bankruptcy a decade earlier. It was filled with the latest printouts of the financial status summary of every one of News Corp's operating companies around the world and was produced by the head office financial team on a weekly basis. When I asked Murdoch how accurate a picture it represented, he conceded it was just a 'snapshot' but one that allowed him to 'spot trends'.

'Here,' he said, indicating a line in a spreadsheet for the *Cairns Post* newspaper, a small regional newspaper company he owned in Far North Queensland. 'Look at how the newsprint costs have risen over the past months. We should be able to use our buying power to keep those down.' Consequently, the publisher of the *Cairns Post* could expect a call, if not from Murdoch himself then from one of his executives, asking him to justify the expense line.

When we dropped Murdoch at the hotel he again said he'd be catching up on the paperwork over the weekend and that there was no need to bother ourselves with having to 'chaperone' him around the city. He disappeared up the hotel elevator with a parting remark that we would catch up Monday morning before heading off for the airport and our Beijing meetings.

Early next morning, as I made my way to the coffee shop for breakfast, I noticed Murdoch at the concierge desk in earnest conversation. I wandered over to see if all was under control and if anything was needed but he sort of waved me away with a 'No, it's fine, it's fine'. So I turned on my heel and left him to it.

Later that afternoon, having spent a good part of the day skulking about the Royal Hong Kong Yacht Club, I returned to the hotel to be accosted by a rather exuberant concierge.

'Mr Dover, Mr Dover,' he spluttered, 'I just wanted to let you know the dinner cruise on the harbour has been arranged and the boat will be ready at 7 p.m.'

Funny, I thought. Murdoch hadn't mentioned anything about a boat on the harbour.

'And the flowers that Mr Murdoch ordered, sir. Can I charge them to your room?'

As it transpired, the weather turned inclement and if there was to have been a cruise, it was cancelled. Nevertheless, the wooing, I sensed, had only just begun.

12

Thanks a Million

For a multi-billionaire businessman heading up arguably the most powerful media empire in the world, Rupert Murdoch was the most unpretentious of international travellers. In his not infrequent sorties from Los Angeles to Hong Kong, and thence Beijing, Murdoch was all but indistinguishable from the myriad of bedraggled transpacific commuters emerging from the airport customs hall.

There was no private jet, no entourage of assistants and minders, no phalanx of bodyguards, no trolley-load of designer label luggage – just 'the boss' with the battered suit bag and briefcase ambling up the arrivals hall with a look of decided embarrassment that you'd bothered to meet him at all.

It was a stark contrast to the arrangements put in place for his Time Warner counterpart and rival at the time, Jerry Levin, on his trips out to China, which I witnessed firsthand a few years later.

Levin's visits were always lavish presidential-style events, preceded by an advance guard of international affairs advisers from head office, a security detail, his chief-of-staff and a band of assistants, which comprised his travelling office. Air clearances were made to allow the company jet (or jets on occasion) to fly direct to Beijing, and fleets of limousines and luggage vans were on hand to transport Levin and troops from the airport VIP guest rooms to the presidential suite at the plushest hotel in town.

In those days Murdoch travelled on his own on a commercial jet – normally United Airlines because News Corp enjoyed a discount. His one concession to luxury was to ask the check-in staff to block the adjacent seat 'if the first class section wasn't full', so he needn't have someone looking over his shoulder as he worked his way through the mountain of paperwork that always accompanied him on his travels. And if we had to squeeze three into the back of the office car sent to meet him, that was fine by him too.

Murdoch always insisted that he didn't need a hotel suite ('Just a room with a desk and personal fax machine will do me fine'), although the hotel would often upgrade him in any case. At the end of a fourteen-hour flight across the Pacific Ocean he would book in for a massage followed by a brisk walk around Kowloon's city streets, full as they were with electronic and clothing outlets. On one occasion, he returned with a large parcel under his arm – it was a suit that had been on sale at a nearby Chinese tailor. A clearly excited Murdoch bragged about what a bargain it was compared to what he normally paid for his hand-tailored outfits back in Los Angeles.

'The Chinese bloke offered to take up the trouser legs and hem them for a small fee, but I declined,' chortled Murdoch. 'I'll just get the hotel butler to do it – he'll sew them for free and I'll save the money!' He was forever in search of a good bargain.

Murdoch would normally turn in by midnight. If the rest of us were having a nightcap at the hotel bar, he might join us for one drink but rarely more than that. At 6 a.m. the following morning he'd be in the gym on an exercise bike, with a television set tuned to CNN. He would be muttering about the network's liberal bias (he was at the time preparing to launch his new Fox News cable network in the US as a counter). Clutched in one hand would be a bundle of faxes that had come in overnight, which he read as the sweat streamed, dripping over the newly arrived updates from the far reaches of his empire. By 8 a.m. he'd be at the office of STAR TV, ready for his first round of meetings. His energy seemed to be boundless and after a week on the road it was you rather than him left absolutely exhausted.

Murdoch's trips to Asia usually involved a full day in Hong Kong to hear progress reports from the STAR TV executives before boarding a scheduled Dragonair flight to Beijing for another round of jousting with the capital's bureaucrats. It was while on the plane from Hong Kong to Beijing that we read the news.

Murdoch was sitting up the front in seat 1A with his usual

screeds of paperwork. I was three rows back, thumbing through a copy of the *South China Morning Post* newspaper. There, on page three, a small article reported that HarperCollins had just announced it would be publishing the memoirs of former Hong Kong Governor Chris Patten.

At this stage I carried the title of Vice President – News Corporation (China). HarperCollins Publishers was a wholly-owned subsidiary of News Corp and the idea of publishing Patten's book had certainly never been mentioned to me. I wondered whether Murdoch had been aware but for reasons best known to himself had decided not to share it. I walked down the aircraft aisle and passed a copy of the newspaper to the boss, pointed out the article and resumed my seat.

Judging from the mumbled oaths, tearing of paper and crumpling of notes, I correctly assumed Murdoch was not aware of the HarperCollins decision either. As we alighted from the plane in Beijing and cleared immigration and customs, he said nothing about it although he was unusually subdued. His only sign of agitation thus far was on the drive in from the airport to the city centre, when he borrowed my mobile and determinedly tried to put a call through to Anthea Disney in New York, who at that time was head of News America Publishing Group, the division which owned HarperCollins. Unable to get her on the line, he left a message in no uncertain terms that she should contact him ASAP.

The General Manager of the China World Hotel had upgraded

Murdoch to the Presidential Suite – a sprawling apartment decked out in Ming Dynasty-style furniture. Having been accompanied by us up to his suite for a brief discussion on the coming day's program, Murdoch instructed Gary Davey and me to order some drinks, including a white wine for himself, while he made some quick phone calls from an adjoining room.

Anthea Disney was getting the 'please explain' from Murdoch. He also wanted to track down Eddie Bell, then Chairman of HarperCollins in London. It was Eddie Bell who had done the book deal with Patten. As far as we could gather while sipping our drinks in the lounge room, a very robust conservation ensued in which the media titan was outlining in rather vivid terms what Bell would later describe in a leaked memo as 'the negative aspects of publication'. What we heard was more akin to 'kill the fuckin' book'.

When he had finished the conversation and moved to join us in the adjoining lounge room, Murdoch was in a decidedly testy mood. A butler had appeared and placed an opened bottle of wine on the table and presented Murdoch with the room service chit to sign. The billionaire media magnate took a long look at the chit and shot a disapproving glance at the wine on offer – an Australian Jacob's Creek chardonnay normally priced at around US$10 in a Sydney wine shop, for which he was being charged US$110. Murdoch scrunched up the chit in front of the astounded butler and ordered him to put the cork back in the bottle and remove it instantly.

'I'm not paying a hundred dollars for that crap – take it back,' he demanded and plopped down in a lounge chair in disgust, leaving all of us somewhat stunned as he sat there in silence, seemingly gnawing on the index finger of his right hand, as was his habit when deep in thought.

There was a certain irony in the Jacob's Creek incident, when a few hours later Murdoch was ushered into the most precocious, over-the-top wine bar Beijing had ever seen. At a time when China's tipple of choice was very much still a glass of locally brewed maotai, this bar had a wine list that topped a million dollars in value and contained rare old vintages from around the world. The bar belonged to Zong Lulu, who, besides being an aspiring film director, was the wife of one of Beijing's then rising business luminaries, Wang Xuebing.

For more than a decade Wang Xuebing had shone as one of the brightest stars in the often dark sky of the Chinese financial world. In 1993 he took over as head of the Bank of China, and two years after that began running another of China's 'Big Four' banks, China Construction Bank (CCB). He was part of an elite cadre of officials singled out by Premier Zhu Rongji and given the task of restructuring China's tottering state-owned financial system.

Through the Bank of China and later the CCB, Wang had provided key loans to Murdoch's Phoenix Television joint venture partner, Liu Changle. It was Liu who had pressured me to put the meeting with Zong Lulu on the agenda. It seemed she had just completed her first full-length feature film and was very keen to meet Murdoch in the hope that his Twentieth Century Fox division might see fit to buy the rights for distribution in the US. We had little interest in the film but thought it might be appropriate to go ahead with the meeting in order to do the right thing by Liu and his financial backers, and also to stay in the good books of Wang, who was close to some – but, as it turned out, not all – of the Chinese leadership.

Murdoch was reluctant to attend but agreed once I'd explained the background to the meeting. However, he was grumpy – tired from his long flight and resulting jet lag, and still internally steamed up about the pending HarperCollins deal with Patten. It was a late, post-dinner meeting and as we turned up to the newly opened wine bar we were greeted by our glamorous host and an entourage of Beijing's artistic elite, which seemed to comprise a number of young men with long hair pulled back, ponytail-style, and a sprinkling of aspiring actresses all too keen to get themselves in front of the 'great movie mogul, Mur-Dock'.

We were directed to a long table and seated on one side with Murdoch in the middle, while our host Zong Lulu sat opposite with her entourage arranged either side of her. She proffered the wine list to Murdoch and asked him to choose something to drink.

Murdoch thumbed through the pages of the menu, stopped at the Australian Wines heading, pointed at one of the listed vintages and snapped it shut. Having witnessed the raised-eyebrows response of the wine waiter, I picked up and opened the wine list to see what Murdoch had ordered. Whether it was because he had forgotten his reading glasses or was just feeling particularly malicious in his grumpiness, Murdoch had selected a 1965 Grange Hermitage at US$3500 a bottle – on his host's tab.

The wines decanted and poured, I was discreetly savouring perhaps the only opportunity I was ever likely to have to taste a rare king of Australian wines, while Zong Lulu proceeded to give us all a long dissertation about her recent film and her Hollywood aspirations. While I attempted to feign at least some interest, Murdoch, who had taken barely a sip of his wine, was literally falling asleep, his head lolling down on his chest. My challenge was to keep the conversation going just long enough for me to finish as much of the wine as possible while propping Murdoch up so he didn't collapse on the table and offend anyone.

Fortunately, Murdoch shook himself back into life, suggested that Zong Lulu send a copy of the film to his office in Los Angeles, then stood up and took his leave with a sort of 'don't call us, we'll call you' promise. He swept out the door. It was a less than gracious exit given our indulgence in a rather expensive bottle of red at our host's expense.

As it transpired we needn't have worried – the Chinese banker turned out to be another dud agent of influence for Murdoch. By January 2002, Wang Xuebing should have been at the pinnacle of financial power, as an official with Cabinet-level rank and an alternate member of the Central Committee of the Communist Party. Unfortunately, besotted by his beautiful but occasionally wayward younger wife, Wang had helped orchestrate a Bank of China loan to Zong Lulu of some US$23 million to fund her film-making and other ventures, including the wine bar. It seems the loan was made without collateral and never repaid. In 2003 Wang was convicted of corruption and sentenced to twelve years' jail. Some wine bar!

During the course of the next forty-eight hours in Beijing, prior to his shuffling off to London, Murdoch declined to elaborate on the HarperCollins issue. He did let slip that he had been aware of the publisher's plan to commission the book by Patten when it was mooted just after the official handover of Hong Kong in July 1997. He said at the time he had made clear to the HarperCollins executives his 'personal opposition to the book' and his 'objections to Patten's views on China'. He had suggested other publishers would almost certainly pick up the book.

The thing about Murdoch is that he very rarely issued directives or instructions to his senior executives or editors. Instead, by way of discussion he would make known his personal viewpoint on a certain matter. What was expected in return, at least from those seeking tenure of any length in the Murdoch Empire, was a sort of 'anticipatory compliance'. One didn't need to be instructed about what to do, one simply knew what was in one's long-term interests.

The frustration for Murdoch on this occasion was that the HarperCollins executives had been neither 'anticipatory' nor 'compliant'. He had been under the impression that the book deal had 'gone away'. So Murdoch was clearly dumbfounded to learn that it had not, and that his own executives were putting so much of the company's China investment at risk.

Murdoch had long been a critic of Patten's term as the last Governor of Hong Kong. He had often remarked that Patten didn't understand China, and (as was true) had not visited the mainland since his arrival to take up his position as the Queen's representative in 1992; therefore he had not witnessed firsthand the remarkable economic transition taking place there. Murdoch hated what he saw as the British imposition of a hierarchical class system on the people of Hong Kong, where there appeared to be one rule for the white colonials and another for local Chinese. He saw it as a great hypocrisy that Governor Patten and the British government, after a hundred years of colonial rule, should at the last minute take such a great and fervent interest in instituting democratic reform in the interests of a people it had previously denied the right to vote.

But the real objection to the publication of the Patten memoirs was rooted in Murdoch's absolute pragmatism, which puts money before any moral ideology. In late 1997 Murdoch felt the Beijing freeze was finally beginning to thaw and that now, four years after the infamous Whitehall Palace speech, the massive investments in buying influence, the kowtowing and the pillorying he

When Michelle Guthrie succeeded James as CEO, STAR pushed the boundaries of China's media laws with the 'unauthorised' Qinghai Satellite TV Station deal. Its discovery led to the quashing of tentative foreign partnership reforms and the re-imposition of strict controls. After Guthrie's replacement in early 2007, Murdoch admitted: 'We don't do very well in China.'

Murdoch was clearly invigorated by his third marriage and has since presented a more youthful, casual appearance.

© Rick Wilking/REUTERS/Picture Media

Evan Agostini/Staff/Getty

The striking new look at the head of the News Corp family. Taking on her first official company role as Chief of Strategy for MySpace China, Wendi has also produced two daughters, Grace and Chloe, adding to the complexity of the Murdoch dynasty – or perhaps delivering its future in China.

had endured were paying off. In the past six months, he had been granted an audience with Vice Premier Zhu Rongji, been a VIP guest at the Hong Kong handover and appointed an official adviser to the new Chinese-imposed administration there, and was at last being granted ministerial access in Beijing.

The Chinese authorities never once raised the issue of the Patten book with Murdoch during his official meetings, nor with me in an unofficial way, which they sometimes did when the Beijing leadership wished to make its views known to the News Corp chairman. The connection between Patten and HarperCollins was simply not on their radar. Murdoch's decision to pull the book from publication was made without consulting any of us working on the ground in China. It was his call, and his alone, because he felt he had no alternative.

Pity that no one at HarperCollins was listening. Despite Murdoch's protestations, the book deal inexorably rolled on. In early January of 1998, Patten delivered the first 70 000 words – or two-thirds – of his promised manuscript to HarperCollins editor Stuart Proffitt, who, despite his position, had not an inkling that the News Corp chairman had already ordered that the book be dumped. When word filtered back to the upper echelons of the Murdoch empire that HarperCollins had not yet even raised the issue of non-publication with Patten, the chatter was that Eddie Bell was either the bravest executive the company had ever had in its employ, or the stupidest. First, he had actually agreed to the commissioning of the book by Patten, and now he appeared to be ignoring Murdoch's express wishes to make it go away.

Murdoch had in fact made it very clear in December to the News America Publishing head, Anthea Disney, that she issue a directive to Bell instructing that HarperCollins relinquish the rights to the Patten book immediately. Understandably, Bell was in an enormous quandary. He was chairman of one of the great publishing houses of the English language – a position that gave him extraordinary sway and prestige in the world of book publishing. Now he was being asked not only to renege on a legal contract but to do so at the cost of the publisher's reputation for editorial independence – and worst of all, to do it to protect his proprietor's commercial interests in China.

Bell continued to procrastinate and even mounted a last-ditch defence of the project. On 20 January, in a memo later leaked to London's *Daily Telegraph* newspaper, the British publisher outlined his concerns about the damage the decision to drop Patten would do to HarperCollins' reputation and warned of the probable critical backlash. He insisted that Disney raise the likely consequences of the action directly with Murdoch in the hope that he might reconsider. Bell seemed to be blithely unaware that the News Corp investment in China now topped US$1 billion and that the business was haemorrhaging financially at the rate of US$100 million a year. Murdoch's curt response was to 'kill the fucking book'.

In China there is a saying that the Emperor's authority stops at the palace gate. Murdoch might have taken heed. For on 29 January not only had HarperCollins failed to halt publication of the Patten book, but it was hosting a reception at the swank Savoy Hotel in London to introduce the former governor to the city's leading booksellers, while heaping praise upon the quality of the upcoming release.

Proffitt, one of the industry's most respected non-fiction editors, described the book as 'enormously impressive and enormously enjoyable'.

'I don't think I have ever read a book by any modern politician which is so lucid or engrossing, or which has quickened my blood so frequently,' the editor told the assembled gathering, adding that it would be a bestseller.

So it must have come as some surprise to Proffitt when on 5 February 1998 he was called in by the HarperCollins management and informed that the publisher was dropping the book because 'the material as it stands does not match up to the original outline or indeed inspire us from a commercial standpoint'.

As was reported at the time, when Proffitt refused to go along with the decision he was handed a legal 'gagging letter' telling him that if he discussed the matter with anyone he would be guilty of gross misconduct and fired without compensation. Proffitt was suspended from his job and in turn launched legal action for breach of contract.

On 10 February, HarperCollins informed Patten that it would

not be publishing his book. As the news began to break around the world, the publishing company launched a spin campaign suggesting the real reasons the book had been dropped were that it had not been up to professional standards and was just plain 'boring'. Patten sued for breach of contract. A gaggle of HarperCollins' most successful authors threatened to walk out in disgust, while Eddie Bell's reputation took the battering he had so recently predicted. But it was Murdoch who copped the most damning criticism of his entire career.

The New York Times called Murdoch's action 'contemptible' and London's *Daily Telegraph* described him as 'the biggest gangster of them all'. *The Financial Times* commented: 'Rupert Murdoch has miscalculated badly. The great media mogul has emerged from the saga of Chris Patten's memoir looking faintly ridiculous . . . We glimpse this modern master of the capitalist universe bent double before the potentates of the people in Beijing.' Murdoch's own media outlets, including the London *Times*, *The Australian*, *New York Post*, Sky News and the Fox News Network, hardly referred to the controversy.

When I asked Murdoch afterwards about whether he'd been stung by the criticism, he simply shrugged it off. 'You develop a thick skin,' he said. 'And in any case I never read what people write about me, I just get on with it. People sometimes point out that such and such article was good or this one bad, but I rarely feel the need to read about myself.'

In Beijing, I tried to make a virtue of Murdoch's bad press and assembled copies of the press cuttings which I hand-delivered to Zeng Jianhui, director of the powerful State Council Information Office (SCIO). Leafing through the cuttings on his desk, even Zeng was astounded by the level of criticism Murdoch had endured in China's interest, shaking his head from side to side and sucking on the back of his teeth. Our Beijing minders were impressed and the Patten incident marked a distinct warming in the relationship with Ding Guangen and the Propaganda Department.

On a personal level, the Patten incident left me questioning for the first time the real cost of accepting the Murdoch dollar and working for News Corporation in China. Pragmatism was one thing but this bordered on the coldly amoral – doing whatever was needed to do to get the deal done.

Murdoch, in an interview with the London *Times* in early March, put the blame for the fiasco squarely at the feet of the HarperCollins executives, claiming they had 'screwed it up' by making excuses for the book's being cancelled and not simply telling Patten – as Murdoch said he had urged last July – 'that there were dozens of other publishers' who would take on the book.

On 6 March 1998 HarperCollins let it be known the company had reached a settlement with Patten and 'unreservedly apologised' to the former Hong Kong governor for any suggestion that his forthcoming book was not up to professional standards. In a media release News Corp reported that the settlement included 'a modest financial sum' but did not reveal further details.

Whatever the sum, it barely matched the value of the publicity Patten garnered out of Murdoch's controversial decision to have the book dropped, virtually guaranteeing it a place on the best-seller list. In October 1998, I met with Patten at a Sydney function hosted by his new publisher, Macmillan, in the basement of a trendy city establishment. After a long chat about the circumstances surrounding the book's launch, I suggested he might like to sign a copy which I would forward to Murdoch.

Patten eagerly obliged, opening a copy of his book and scribbling a message on the flyleaf:

'Dear Rupert, Thanks a million. Warm regards, Chris Patten.'

I sent it on to Murdoch, but I never did receive an acknowledgement.

13

Drowning, Not Waving

While Rupert Murdoch's reputation was being tarnished by the scathing rebukes unleashed by the Western liberal media over his handling of the Patten affair, in China his star was most definitely on the rise, thanks in no small part to the country's most influential film critic, President Jiang Zemin.

In early March 1998, with the connivance of Phoenix chairman Liu Changle's contacts in the SCIO, we had been able to arrange a private showing of the Twentieth Century Fox blockbuster *Titanic* to the Chinese leader and a few of his inner circle. James Cameron's three-hour tale of a rich girl and poor boy who meet on the ill-fated voyage of the 'unsinkable' *Titanic* was already breaking box-office records around the world and getting extraordinary publicity, even in China. Jiang was an avid movie fan and had previously cited among his favourites such Hollywood classics as *Gone with the Wind*, *Waterloo Bridge* and *A Song to Remember*, which he saw during his school years prior to the Cultural Revolution.

Emerging from the viewing, the President told the local media that he would recommend the entire Politburo see it.

'There is this movie called *Titanic*. It cost US$250 million to make, and has cleared US$1 billion in revenues by now. Call it venture investment.

'The movie gives a vivid and thorough portrait of the relationships between the wealthy and the poor, between money and love, and human reactions in a crisis,' he said.

We immediately made a copy of the film available to the Politburo, with a note from Murdoch, so it could be shown inside the leadership compound at Zhongnanhai. I also organised a private screening for government ministers and invited guests at a Beijing cinema. Jiang's endorsement ensured that when the film officially opened in China in early May it went on to be the highest-grossing foreign film ever released in the country. The world's media interpreted the President's favourable review as another sign that Murdoch had further ingratiated himself with the Chinese leadership.

But when Jiang expounded on his comments in an article published in *People's Daily* a few days after the initial screening, it appeared that he had something else in mind:

'I invite my comrades of the Politburo to see the movie – not to propagate capitalism but to better understand our opposition,

158

the better to enable us to succeed. Don't fool ourselves that we are the only ones who know how to create propaganda to our own end.'

Jiang's observations about *Titanic* then were less about the film itself than about the techniques, special effects and characterisations which had produced a story of enormous worldwide appeal. He was pointing out how far the state-controlled media had fallen behind their Western rivals and how much it had to do to in order to make itself relevant. If the state were to stand a chance of winning the propaganda war against the social evils promulgated by Western cultural imperialism, then China's film industry would need to emulate Hollywood, and do so quickly. Jiang's endorsement was less a favourable critique than it was a wake-up call to his own government.

Murdoch, however, was buoyed by the Chinese President's remarks, which seemed to present News Corp in a more favourable light than had been the case in the past. Coming on top of the severe verbal beating he had endured in the West over the Patten fiasco, he felt certain that should he pay another visit to Beijing, Jiang would assent to an audience and the issue of the satellite ban would be resolved. Murdoch was insistent on travelling to Beijing in June and would not be dissuaded. He was convinced his rivals Jerry Levin at Time Warner and Sumner Redstone at Viacom had stolen a march on him and that those of us representing his interests in China were either not sufficiently connected or just not pushing hard enough.

The pressure was on me, as the nominal News Corp representative in China, to arrange the meeting. Murdoch was going to up the ante on this occasion by bringing with him as high-powered a company delegation as was possible, including Peter Chernin, the News Corp Chief Operating Officer who also oversaw Twentieth Century Fox. Les Hinton, the Chairman of News International, would join them from London, and Gary Davey from Hong Kong. Wendi Deng would also be part of the official party.

My contacts at the Foreign Ministry believed a meeting with Jiang might be possible but were not prepared to confirm one. The final call, they argued, would be made by Ding Guangen, and he had his own strategy for dealing with the News Corp chairman. Murdoch was incessant with his phone calls to both Davey and myself, demanding to know if we had confirmation. I told him it was possible – knowing full well it had become improbable. But no one, including me, liked to be the bearer of bad news where Murdoch was concerned.

When the News Corp entourage did arrive, Murdoch was irritable and grumpy. The program that we had arranged was an indication of how far he had come since being placed on the Beijing blacklist five years earlier. Where he had previously been denied access to the senior government officials, the ministers were now lining up to meet with him. The Minister for the State Administration of

Radio, Film and Television (SARFT), the President of CCTV, the President of *People's Daily* . . . but it was the Minister for Education, Chen Zili, who ended up on the receiving end of an intemperate outburst from Murdoch.

Chen was talking about the challenges of utilising satellite technology for educational purposes in China's remote communities, when Murdoch angrily interrupted: 'Look, I don't know why you don't just stop all this nonsense and just lift the ban on satellite dishes and allow us to broadcast in here. We're not going to broadcast news or information that is going to upset anyone. We just want to provide movies and entertainment – and education, medicine, all that we can do for you as well. But let's just get on with it. What else do you want from me?'

The Education Minister sat stunned. Although he didn't speak English and therefore didn't catch the meaning of what Murdoch had said, he could clearly see his guest was agitated. The interpreter remained silent. I leant over and whispered to Murdoch, reminding him that this was the Education Minister – he had no say over satellite landing rights. He just shook his head in frustration and rolled his eyes. The meeting came to a quick end.

Murdoch's last meeting of his trip was not with Jiang Zemin, as he hoped, but Ding Guangen and his minions from the SCIO, Minister Zeng Jianghui and Li Bing. Compared to the formality and posturing of the first meeting between the two men just ten months earlier, the atmosphere on this occasion was positively warm and effusive. Murdoch presented Ding with a catalogue of classic movies taken from the Twentieth Century Fox vaults, plus a DVD copy of *Titanic*. The Propaganda Chief in turn praised Murdoch for his efforts in 'cooperating with the Chinese media and helping present China objectively to the outside world'.

Ding went on to say that 'on this occasion it would not be possible to schedule a meeting with President Jiang Zemin'. Murdoch visibly slumped in his seat at the news. However, the Propaganda Chief went on to say that as a result of the contribution News Corp had made in China, it had been decided by the Chinese authorities that the company would be allowed to open a 'representative office' in Beijing, the first of any foreign media company operating in China. It was an enormous concession by Ding, and a quite extraordinary milestone for Murdoch given his blacklisting five years earlier. He was back in the fold, and ahead of the pack of rival broadcasters that had been nipping at his heels.

But Murdoch was not listening and did not grasp the import of what Ding had said in relation to the representative office. He was still convinced that if he could just meet with Jiang, all could be resolved.

Two weeks later, I was summoned to Hong Kong for a meeting with Davey. The news from Murdoch was that we were both to be replaced by his new handpicked executive for all of Asia – Gareth Chang, who had previously headed DIRECTV's international operations. I returned to Australia to head News Corp's internet arm,

News Interactive, so for a while I was no longer directly involved in Murdoch's China play. Two years later, in 2001, I was recruited to head the Asia-Pacific television and internet operations of the Time Warner subsidiary CNN International, based in Hong Kong. It was an excellent vantage point from which to observe Murdoch's continued machinations across the border in China.

Murdoch's decision to hire the DIRECTV executive had been a long time in the pipeline. He had in fact been courting Chang since the previous December, when he had seen reports quoting the debonair 55-year-old Chinese-American as suggesting that the Hughes International subsidiary DIRECTV was on the verge of breaking into the China market, ahead of STAR TV. On paper, Chang looked to have an impeccable pedigree – the son of a Kuomintang general, he escaped as a boy from Sichuan to Hong Kong in the 1950s before moving to the US West Coast.

A brilliant scholar, Chang graduated from California State University with a BA in mathematics and physics and Doctor of Science, before completing an MBA at Pepperdine University. He became a pin-up boy for his community, being named Outstanding Personality by the Organisation of Chinese-Americans, as well as International Citizen of the Year by the State of California. Prior to being signed up by Murdoch, Chang was Corporate Senior Vice President of Hughes Electronics, President of Hughes International and Executive Chairman of DIRECTV Japan. Before Hughes, he had been Corporate Vice President of McDonnell Douglas Asia/Pacific, and at the time of his appointment to STAR TV Chang was also on the board of Apple Computers and the advisory board of Nike Inc.

Murdoch was totally convinced that the square-jawed and open-faced Chang, with his brush-cut, steely grey hair and penchant for Mandarin jackets, would be the answer to his problems in China. He was also getting much more personal advice from Wendi Deng, who was spending a good deal more time with the company chairman since the announcement in 1998 of a formal separation between Murdoch and Anna, his wife of thirty-one years. Wendi too was of the belief that only someone of Chinese extraction could deal satisfactorily with the Beijing leadership. Chang encouraged the line of thinking in his discussions with Murdoch, and would argue that business in China was about relationships, adding: 'You've got to understand the people involved. It takes a formal and an informal interaction, a balance of the two. Westerners have a great deal of difficulty with this.'

Chang was so smugly confident in his own ability he had all but guaranteed to Murdoch that within two years STAR TV's problems would be resolved and the company would be well on its way to profitability. He was convinced that the Beijing leadership would welcome the presence of 'Chinese face' in News Corporation and that the two sides would be able to sit down and negotiate in a way that would never have been possible with a Western 'foreign devil' in charge. Murdoch was so taken by the stylish Chang's ambitious claims of being able to turn STAR TV from a ruinous loss-maker into a profitable powerhouse, that he appointed him not just to the position of Executive Chairman of STAR TV, but also as a Director of the News Corporation board, as well as to the company's Executive Committee, with responsibility for all News Corp activities in Asia. It was, as Murdoch would later acknowledge, one of the most generous remuneration packages he has personally negotiated.

Murdoch made the announcement with great fanfare. 'Mr Chang is an outstanding international executive with a distinguished career in technology, systems and television platform management,' he said in the official press release. 'The company is excited about the progress we have made in Asia through STAR TV. Mr Chang's appointment is recognition of the many new challenges and opportunities which lie ahead.'

In Beijing, the SCIO was confounded by the Murdoch decision to appoint Chang. It felt that after years of suspicion and mistrust it had finally been able to establish a working relationship with News Corp via Liu Changle at Phoenix, Gary Davey in Hong Kong and myself in Beijing. It was not that they disliked the new Executive Chairman; they'd just had no exposure to him. It had taken several years to develop the current level of trust and understanding between the two sides and now Murdoch was inserting a completely new factor into the equation. In their minds, News Corp was particularly well-placed compared to its rivals as they had bent over backwards to try to accommodate Murdoch's ambitions, even if this was at their timing and pace.

The Chinese felt Liu was their trusted conduit to Murdoch – he was one of them, he understood the system within which they worked, he knew the limits of the boundaries he could push and he was inside the Murdoch camp. Moreover, if push came to shove, Liu could be 'relied upon' to do the right thing. Chang, on the other hand, was at best a Chinese-American who had grown up in the US outside the confines of the Communist Party and Chinese mainland culture. As much as Chang would profess his 'Chinese-ness' in Beijing, they would refer to him as a 'banana – yellow on the outside, white on the inside'. His appointment threatened Beijing's investment in Phoenix and its means of controlling Murdoch's entry into China. Murdoch's appetite, they mused at the time, 'appeared insatiable'.

Chang took up his appointment on 1 September 1998. Three months later, on 10 December, true to its word the SCIO arranged the long-awaited meeting between President Jiang Zemin and Rupert Murdoch – although insisting that along with the STAR TV Executive Chairman Chang, Liu Changle should also be present. Jiang made a point of greeting Liu effusively as the News Corp delegation entered the Zhongnanhai meeting room. This, the first meeting between the Chinese leader and the feared media tycoon, was a fairly formal affair, although the sentiments expressed by Jiang, and widely reported in the national media two days later, were a clear sign that Murdoch had been well and truly rehabilitated.

Jiang offered his 'appreciation for the efforts made by world media mogul Rupert Murdoch in reporting on China objectively and cooperating with the Chinese press over the past two years'. The remark notably excluded Murdoch's earlier attempts to court favour by ingratiating himself with the Deng family and circumventing the authority of the Propaganda Department and the SCIO.

'China has made remarkable achievements not only in economic construction, but in the media and culture as well,' Jiang added. 'Exchanges between China and the rest of the international community have been constantly increasing, and China needs to reinforce its links with other countries to promote mutual understanding and cooperation. The news media play a very important role in boosting mutual understanding between China and the rest of the world and we welcome the News Corporation efforts to promote China to the world.'

Murdoch, well aware he should not push his business interests too hard on his first meeting, responded by expressing 'News and STAR TV's willingness to expand cooperation with [his] Chinese counterparts in co-production and broadcasting internationally, and to build on existing cooperative technical projects to contribute to the development of this sector of the media industry'.

He went on to express his 'admiration for China's tremendous achievements in every field over the past two decades', and told Jiang that he was 'willing to further enhance friendly cooperation to present the world with a better understanding of China'.

The meeting with Jiang coincided with the official approval

of the News Corporation Representative Office in Beijing, which had been mooted by Ding the previous July. At a ceremony to mark its opening, the new STAR TV head, Chang, opined that the company wanted to develop more 'TV programming inside the mainland, from sports to costume drama series'. Over the next few months Chang would continue to make bold pronouncements about News Corp's aspirations, which covered everything from launching a major baseball league in China, to buying one of the nation's leading football teams, entering into movie production deals with six Chinese film studios, and the co-production of children's programming and comedies.

But Chang's ambitious undertaking to Murdoch, that he could 'deliver China' and turn STAR TV's fortunes around, appeared to be making no headway. Despite Murdoch's meeting with the Chinese leadership there had been no change to the ban on satellite dishes, nor had STAR TV been granted any additional access to the country's cable systems. Inside both STAR TV and News Corp there was also a growing appreciation that Chang was struggling to come to terms with the operational side of running a major media business. His background prior to joining News Corp had largely been on the technical side of the satellite business. He employed a number of his old Hughes cronies in key positions at the new Beijing Representative Office, but his STAR TV colleagues began to complain privately that the new boss appeared to have no strategy other than throwing money at spurious programming ideas. STAR

TV was still unable to collect subscription revenues in China and advertisers were still reluctant to come on board with a broadcaster that could provide only limited official access to the mainstream Chinese audience. Chang, they said, could 'talk the talk, but not walk the walk'.

James Murdoch and Wendi Deng also began to pass through Hong Kong regularly as part of News Corp's new media strategy, looking at acquisition targets in China and India for its growing stable of internet properties, and would often meet with Chang to discuss their plans. By the end of 1999, both of them were reporting back to Murdoch that there were serious problems in the executive ranks at STAR TV and, of more concern, they doubted Chang's ability to deliver on his promises.

In early 2000 STAR TV found itself embroiled in a battle for the control of Cable & Wireless HKT, Hong Kong's leading telecommunications operator, with Richard Li, Chief Executive of internet investment company Pacific Century CyberWorks (PCCW). Ironically, Li had founded PCCW on the proceeds of the sale of STAR TV to Murdoch seven years earlier. STAR had plans for a joint venture with HKT to offer interactive television and high-speed internet access. But PCCW's Li had made an audacious bid for HKT to thwart a rival offer from Singapore Telecommunications (SingTel). Murdoch had little interest in working with the PCCW team if it successfully acquired the Hong Kong telco, feeling he had been badly burnt in the original STAR TV deal – in which Li had been less than forthcoming about the real level of commitment from advertisers, and used this to ramp up the purchase price. Chang was under considerable pressure from Murdoch to prevent the PCCW offer from proceeding. The STAR TV Executive Chairman was confident his *guanxi* in Beijing and Hong Kong would be enough to stifle the deal.

In an effort to boost the chances of PCCW's rival, Murdoch agreed to invest US$1 billion into SingTel, should its bid be successful, thereby enabling the company to raise its bid for HKT. As a result, the SingTel CEO Lee Hsien Yang, a son of Singapore's founding Prime Minister Lee Kuan Yew, flew to London to present the improved offer to the Cable and Wireless board. Murdoch, buoyed by Chang's confidence, was convinced he had backed a winner. But at the last minute the 33-year-old Li managed to out-manoeuvre Murdoch by getting four banks, including HSBC Holdings and the Bank of China, to lend him a further US$1 billion – a record in Hong Kong at the time – to clinch the deal.

On the day PCCW won the right to buy HKT, News Corp announced that STAR TV Executive Chairman Gareth Chang had 'resigned to explore other business opportunities'. It was not just the HKT deal that had brought Chang undone. He had clearly overestimated his own ability to deliver for Murdoch. Chang was well-connected in Beijing, but he failed to grasp the political sensitivities involved in grappling with the Propaganda Department and the SCIO. He had also demonstrated an almost dismissive attitude to the new India market, which Murdoch and his son James now increasingly viewed as offering far more potential than China in terms of access for satellite television broadcasting. Wendi, who in her travels to China with stepson James to clinch a myriad of internet deals had come into more regular contact with Chang, had started to doubt whether the STAR CEO had in fact any clear vision for opening up the China market for Murdoch, apart from self-aggrandisement. She had made her views known to her husband.

Just eighteen months after Murdoch had announced Chang's appointment to STAR TV, the News Corp board and the company's Executive Committee, he was gone – from all positions. STAR TV's access to the China market remained unchanged. Murdoch's only public comment on the departure of his handpicked would-be saviour: 'It didn't work out. We had to move on.'

In Chang's place, Murdoch announced that News Corp's Co-Chief Operating Officer Chase Carey and Executive Vice President James Murdoch had been appointed interim Co-Chairmen of STAR TV. Bruce Churchill, STAR's Deputy Chief Executive Officer and Chief Operating Officer, would assume day-to-day operational responsibility, reporting to Carey and James.

At the SCIO in Beijing they just rolled their eyes and shook their heads in disbelief. The Chinese value stability over upheaval, continuity over change. They famously claim it is 'a curse to be born in interesting times'. Murdoch, in the eyes of the Beijing leadership, was doing his best to make their lives interesting.

14

London Calling

Just how extraordinary had been the journey of the Guangzhou factory manager's daughter was never more evident than on the balmy autumn afternoon of 21 October 1999, inside the main entrance of London's renowned British Museum. There at the very front of the reception line stood media tycoon Rupert Murdoch and his new wife of just four months, Wendi Deng Murdoch, nervously awaiting the arrival of their guests – Her Majesty Queen Elizabeth II of the United Kingdom and the President of China, Jiang Zemin.

Rupert and Wendi had been married on 25 June, seventeen days after Murdoch's divorce came through from his second wife, Anna. The ceremony took place aboard the *Morning Glory* on the Hudson River in New York – fittingly, perhaps, in view of the Statue of Liberty and Ellis Island. Only eighty-two people – among them family members and friends, including American junk bond king Michael

Milken and Russian entrepreneur Boris Berezovsky – attended the private service, which sailed from Chelsea Piers with a string ensemble playing Mozart, conducted by New York Supreme Court Justice Jacqueline Silbermann. Welsh singing prodigy Charlotte Church performed three songs at the wedding.

For anyone who saw the couple together after the marriage, there was little doubt Wendi had inaugurated a second youth in Murdoch. Despite a bout with prostate cancer, Murdoch's energy levels, which had always been admirable, seemed higher than ever. The British Museum event was in fact a sort of official 'coming out' for Wendi, who had up until that time been content to take a lower-key role running the couple's private life rather than being involved in the everyday grind of business. She was, after all, still finding her feet as the wife of one of the most feared and respected media tycoons in the world. But here in London her Chinese-language skills would be an enormous asset in the banter with the head of the world's fastest-growing economy.

It was no coincidence that Murdoch stood at the front of the welcoming queue of some 300 of London's cultural elite. He had seen to it that the News Corporation-owned London *Times* had been the major sponsor of 'Gilded Dragons – Buried Treasures From China's Golden Ages', an exhibition of artefacts never before seen outside China to mark President Jiang's historic visit to the United Kingdom, the first ever by a Chinese head of state. Jiang had in fact insisted that apart from his official duties, a variety of cultural trips be part of his program, including a Shakespeare play in rehearsal at the Globe, the replica of the Bard's theatre; an 'old Britain' trip down the river Thames to the Royal Observatory in Greenwich; a visit to the embodiment of Tony Blair's new Britannia, the Millennium Dome; and a day trip to Cambridge.

Now, as Jiang entered the Great Hall of the British Museum accompanied by Queen Elizabeth and Prince Philip for the joint opening ceremony, he immediately recognised the familiar face of Murdoch, moved towards him and grabbed his outstretched hand in a long and vigorous handshake, with much grinning and nodding from both participants. Murdoch then turned to his wife, who two years earlier had been an intern at STAR TV's Hong Kong headquarters, and introduced her to President Jiang. Next were the Queen and Prince Philip – the handshakes noticeably limper and shorter, although Her Majesty stopped briefly to congratulate Wendi on her recent nuptials.

It was little wonder Murdoch cut a now familiar figure to Jiang – it was the third time in two days he had been introduced to the world's most powerful media tycoon. Murdoch had been present at a state banquet the previous evening hosted by the Queen at Buckingham Palace. Indeed, just prior to the official opening of the 'Gilded Dragons' exhibition Jiang had come from a small private luncheon hosted by Prime Minister Tony Blair at the official residence, 10 Downing Street, where the guests had included Peter Stothard of *The Times*, Sir John Birt, outgoing director general of the BBC, Lord Hollick, Chief Executive of United News and Media, and Murdoch.

Blair, who still owed Murdoch for his newspapers' backing during the recent British elections and who was well aware of his benefactor's vast business interests in China, ensured that the media proprietor had the seat of honour, next to Jiang. Downing Street was strangely coy about the lunch at the time, refusing to reveal the menu and only grudgingly providing the names of some of those present, claiming the discussions were mostly about bilateral relations – an odd choice, given the place of honour accorded to the American-Australian Murdoch. Jiang would have yet another opportunity to exchange views with Murdoch later the same evening, at the return state banquet at the Chinese Embassy, where the media tycoon was again on the VIP guest list. Murdoch was proving inseparable from the Chinese visitor.

Fawning over the President of China and Chairman of the Chinese Communist Party had become something of pastime for the world's leading media tycoons during the autumn of 1999. Indeed, spending valuable 'face time' with Jiang Zemin had spurred a virtual rivalry between Murdoch and his Time Warner counterpart, Jerry Levin, who just three weeks prior to the presidential visit to Britain had boasted about having entertained the Chinese leader at 'breakfast, lunch and dinner' during his *Fortune* magazine-sponsored 'Global Forum' event in Shanghai. The conference, sponsored by Time Warner, and coinciding with the fiftieth anniversary of the founding of the People's Republic of China, was attended by some 300 CEOs of major multinationals and forty Chinese government ministers and provincial governors, at the newly opened US$1.6 billion international airport in Shanghai's Pudong development area. More than fifty private jets had touched down in time for forum participants to view a thirty-minute fireworks spectacular over the Huangpu River, prior to the opening gala dinner in the brand-new US$100 million international convention centre.

Levin, introducing his 'good friend' President Jiang Zemin to the assembled guests, noted that he was someone with whom he had 'been privileged to spend considerable time . . . an experience made memorable by his sincerity, openness and thoughtful insights'. The Time Warner CEO would later present Jiang with a bust of US President Abraham Lincoln, whom the Chinese leader greatly admired. In fact, Jiang had a penchant for reciting the entire Gettysburg Address off by heart.

In response, during his keynote speech to the forum, President Jiang threatened force against Taiwan and warned that comments by the West on China's internal matters (namely human rights) were not welcome.

'We oppose any efforts by any country to impose its own social system and ideology on another country,' he noted.

At the same conference, Sumner Redstone, the Chairman of Viacom, and a Global Forum delegate, made it clear he agreed with

Jiang's pronouncements and that his rock music video channel MTV would not challenge China's Communist authorities.

'You can rest assured we are not going to take any action with respect to our content that is displeasing to the Chinese government,' he told the conference.

Redstone would later add: 'We do not view it as our role to tell the government of China how to run China. We want to do business. We cannot succeed in China without being a friend of the Chinese people and the Chinese government.'

Ironically, as Levin was waxing lyrical about the virtues of Jiang and China's new openness, the Beijing authorities had banned a *Time* magazine edition marking the country's fiftieth anniversary. The edition, whose masthead was emblazoned with the headline 'China's Amazing Half-Century', fell foul of Chinese censors for including articles written by exiled dissidents Wei Jingsheng and Wang Dan, as well as the Tibetan Dalai Lama. *Time* had planned to deliver complimentary copies of the 27 September issue to the 300 foreign CEOs, who also included Steve Case from AOL, Jack Welch of General Electric Co. and the head of Dell Computer, Michael Dell. China pulled the magazine from hotel newsstands and other retail outlets, allowing delivery only of subscriber copies. Levin made no mention of the ban during his public comments at the forum.

Murdoch, on the other hand, had left the Beijing authorities in no doubt where he stood on Tibet and the Dalai Lama. In an interview with his biographer, William Shawcross, published in *Vanity Fair* magazine and released in the newsstands during the first week of September, Murdoch famously declared of the Dalai Lama: 'I have heard cynics who say he's a very political old monk shuffling around in Gucci shoes.'

Commenting on Tibet before the Chinese occupation in 1950, Murdoch added: 'It was a pretty terrible old autocratic society out of the Middle Ages . . . Maybe I'm falling for their [China's] propaganda, but it was an authoritarian medieval society without any basic services.'

The comments went down particularly well with the Beijing authorities but caused a furore elsewhere as human rights groups and civil libertarians accused him of 'ignorance' and of being a 'propagandist for China's rulers'. To be fair to Murdoch, and I had engaged in conversations about Tibet with him a number of times the previous year, his comments were less a defence of the Chinese invasion and occupation than a criticism of a monastic, medieval feudalism that had impoverished a great many peasants, and which in reality had always been a far cry from the Shangri-La portrayed by Hollywood and a good deal of the Western media.

Nevertheless, the timing of Murdoch's comments appeared pragmatically chosen, given that the media coverage occurred during Jiang's official visit to Australia in early September 1999, when he could not but have noticed the headlines in the local media. In Beijing, the SCIO, which had been tasked with countering the

external public relations efforts of the Dalai Lama and his supporters, were even more grateful for the remarks by the powerful media
tycoon. If Wendi Deng's transformation had been miraculous, then
so too had the journey of Murdoch from outright pariah to trusted
ally of China's Propaganda Department. In reality, Murdoch had
all but resolved his political differences with his former Chinese
antagonists. He was on first-name terms with President Jiang and
as far as the SCIO was concerned, the 'welcome mat' was well and
truly out whenever the media mogul wanted to visit Beijing.

But if Murdoch believed the new political reality would result
in some change to the regime which still banned the use of satellite receiver dishes and restricted STAR TV to three-star or better
hotels and official compounds, he was mistaken. Having overcome
the political hurdles that had confronted him to date, Murdoch
now faced a new obstruction – vested commercial interests. While
he was no longer seen as a political threat, the Chinese television
broadcasters saw him as an absolute commercial threat to their own
financial viability and they lobbied voraciously that the restrictions
on Murdoch's access to the living rooms of China remain firmly
in place.

Like so many other Western businessmen, Murdoch had been
lured to China by the prospect of one billion potential customers.
But the Chinese authorities have always jealously guarded their
own backyard. The Chinese market is for the Chinese. Citing
'the national interest', the major Chinese broadcasters, including

CCTV, the Shanghai Media Group and Guangzhou Cable TV, complained that with his massive financial resources and technical know-how Murdoch would swamp the Chinese market, absorbing a vast share of the television advertising spending and leaving the domestic operators picking over the remnants. They needed time to be in a position to compete with the media barbarians at the gates to China – time to raise capital, invest in new technologies and gain expertise, even if it meant copying and emulating their Western rivals.

To this end, the State Administration of Radio, Film and Television (SARFT) had by 2000 decreed that cable, not satellite, would be the predominant means of pay television distribution in China. Cable meant distribution could be simply and immediately controlled with a good pair of wire cutters, not the intangible wireless signal beamed from a satellite far out of reach and in the hands of a foreign operator. It also meant that any foreign broadcaster would be forced through a single Chinese-controlled distribution point in order to get carriage on the cable systems. And you could make the foreign broadcaster pay for the privilege. The idea of being both gatekeeper and toll collector was a very good one. In fact it had been espoused on numerous occasions by Murdoch himself in his discussions with the head of SARFT and CCTV – except, in his vision, he saw News Corp and the Chinese authorities operating in partnership and sharing the revenues. The SARFT hierarchy, many of whom had been provided with all-expenses-paid trips to the UK to see the BSkyB platform in operation, loved the Murdoch concept and set about implementing it. They just excluded Murdoch from his own plan.

It seemed not to have occurred to Murdoch that China, like the US, Europe and Australia, might want to restrict foreign broadcasters from having unfettered access to its market. Murdoch's approach to China up to this point was steeped in a sort of colonial mindset – that somehow the Chinese would welcome a white man bearing gifts, in this case Western-style television entertainment programming, in exchange for allowing him to pillage the country of its resources, namely television subscribers and advertising revenues. He seemed genuinely perplexed that having proved himself a trusted political friend of China, the Chinese simply didn't now open up its market to the full array of his STAR TV channels.

Murdoch had hoped with STAR TV to replicate the success of BSkyB, made possible because of the cosy relationship he enjoyed with Britain's political Establishment, coupled with BSkyB's monopoly position in what had been an underserved market. Unlike the US, Britain and Australia, the Chinese leadership was not in a position where it had to face the polls, and consequently it didn't need the support of the Murdoch media to sway the voters come election-time. In China, Murdoch had no such direct means of currying favour with the leadership. Without their blessing he was unable to collect subscriptions or even advertising revenue inside China. In the UK, he had been both gatekeeper and toll collector for BSkyB, charging third-party channels a hefty fee for carriage on his monopoly platform. In China he had been out-manoeuvred by the Chinese to the point where the tables had been turned. And while China may have been vastly under-served in the past by its domestic media, that was rapidly changing.

Yet for all that, STAR TV was still a very sizeable business. By 2000, it comprised thirty broadcast services in seven languages, potentially reaching some 300 million viewers in fifty-three Asian countries. The problem for Murdoch was that the market seemed to fail to recognise its own potential and in many ways the Asian broadcaster had become a millstone around the neck of the News Corp share price. At a time when exuberance for tech stocks – and the so-called 'dot coms' in particular – had pushed stock markets to record highs, the News Corp stock languished far behind its rivals in relevant terms. One can imagine Murdoch's horror at the news of 11 January 2000, when America Online, the pioneer of dial-up internet access, acquired Time Warner, the world's largest media company. The acquisition was symbolic of the dot coms' challenge to 'old media' companies. Murdoch was convinced News Corp not only had the technology assets, but also proven business models in its portfolio of corporations – the market just didn't recognise this and had instead consigned the company to the 'old media' bin.

Concerned that News Corp, a company he had built into a media empire spanning six continents, might easily go the way of Time Warner, Murdoch devised a plan to spin-off a new entity – Sky

Global – which would be a holding company for all of his satellite and technology interests around the world. The new company would include his 38 per cent stake in BSkyB plus STAR TV, his various Latin American pay TV interests, and the digital technology division NDS with its stake in US interactive TV company GemStar, as well as being a stalking horse for his long-coveted goal of acquiring the missing piece of his global empire, US satellite broadcaster DIRECTV. Aiming to take advantage of the voracious appetite for tech stock in the US financial markets, Murdoch hoped to raise as much as US$40 billion in a partial float by the end of 2000.

Whereas previously the success of BSkyB was seen as the lynchpin of the Sky Global offering, by March 2000 Murdoch and his offsiders became convinced that the untapped potential of STAR TV would be the major selling point. It was Richard Li, who had successfully stolen the Cable & Wireless Hong Kong Telecom (HKT) deal from under News Corp's nose, who now prompted the change of direction. Richard Li's company PCCW had been a minor player in the internet sector prior to its audacious bid for HKT, which would scuttle the deal STAR TV had made to provide content to HKT's proposed new broadband network. News of the HKT deal, and the market's appetite in particular for China technology plays, saw PCCW's share price hit a record HK$131.75, pitching it from near obscurity to become the eighth-largest Hong Kong company by capitalisation.

With Sky Global now in play, Murdoch also needed to

convince the market that STAR TV, rather than being the poor cousin of the media empire, was in fact going to be its salvation. The key was a change in strategic direction that would see STAR TV, in Murdoch's words, 'migrate from a pay television service to become Asia's premier multimedia, broadband platform'. He also needed to convince the market he was serious. Having sacked his rainmaker, STAR TV Chairman and Chief Executive Gareth Chang, from his positions in late January, Murdoch needed to come up with a new name that would convince the market that STAR TV was indeed a crucial part of News Corp and the potential centrepiece of the Sky Global float. And so he did. The name was Murdoch – James Murdoch.

15

Little Murdoch

Chinese astrology dictates that James Murdoch, born as he was on 13 December 1972, would be a Rat. The attributes of those people born in the Year of the Rat, the first sign of the Chinese zodiac, make them excellent leaders, pioneers and conquerors. Charming, passionate, charismatic, practical and hardworking, Rats are also considered the most organised and systematic of the twelve signs. They are, according to the traditional portents, highly ambitious and strong-willed people who are keen and unapologetic promoters of their own agendas.

On his appointment to the position of Chairman and Chief Executive Officer of STAR TV, on 31 May 2000, it was clear that the younger Murdoch would need to demonstrate all of his Rat attributes if he was going to make this post a winner. At twenty-seven years of age he had been interim co-Chairman of STAR TV, along with Chase Carey, since his father had ousted Gareth Chang from the position. But with the Sky Global float now on the agenda, and STAR TV elevated to be a vital piece of the offering, James had been tapped by his father to go to Hong Kong and try to put some gloss on the hitherto failing Asian satellite broadcaster.

It was a very challenging assignment for James Murdoch, the first time he had been placed in a very high-profile and equally accountable executive position within the News Corp empire after none-too-stellar beginnings as an aspiring media tycoon. Interestingly, the announcement of the appointment was made by the President and Chief Operating Officer of News Corp, Peter Chernin, and not Murdoch senior, who was recuperating from prostate cancer treatment at the time, and taking time out from the office if not from work itself. In the announcement Chernin made note of the 'exceptional job' James had done 'overseeing the company's worldwide new media strategy over the past year'. In hindsight those comments would be made to look a bit premature.

Although born in England to Rupert and Anna, James had become a US citizen after moving to New York as a toddler. He attended Horace Mann School in New York City and graduated in 1991 before taking up studies at Harvard University. At Harvard, he majored in visual arts and became an editor of the satirical magazine *The Harvard Lampoon*. He dropped out of Harvard school just prior to his senior year and spent several months following the Grateful Dead before setting up Rawkus, the record label he later sold to the family business. As part of the lure to get James back inside the family tent, Murdoch senior not only arranged for News Corp to purchase Rawkus, but made his youngest son chairman of the company's Australian music label Festival Records – somewhat to the astonishment of the Australian music industry. James took to the new position at Festival with gusto, restructuring the label's management team, and convincing the company to acquire a 51 per cent stake in rival Mushroom Records, which he then merged to create Festival Mushroom Records (FMR). This was to be the first step in creating a new international entertainment company. But even as he did so, James Murdoch was taking an increasing interest in an entirely new media platform – the internet. His responsibilities were expanded and he took on the role of Vice President for News Corp in charge of new media and music in the US.

By 1997 James was scheduled to become deputy publisher at the *New York Post*, the money-losing daily newspaper dear to his father's interests. But showing he had something other than ink in his veins, James resisted his father's overtures, opting instead to remain head of the newly formed News America Digital Publishing (NADP). He oversaw the development of the company's entertainment portal iGuide, its purchase of financial website *The Street* and the short-lived online music site *Whammo*. But perhaps the most defining moment was his avid pursuit of News Corp's near-disastrous US$450 million bid for the once-vaunted deans of push technology, Pointcast. Fortunately for James and the company, the deal fizzled when the Pointcast management team spurned the offer – only to be sold a year later for just US$7 million to another company.

But within News Corp, James was the one largely credited with reigniting his father's interest in the internet at a time when the other major media companies were rapidly expanding their online presence. In 1999 he was put in charge of News Corp's new media strategy worldwide, as the corporation went on a massive spending spree, playing catch-up as the internet bubble continued to inflate at a rapid rate. In late 1999 and early 2000, he and his new stepmother, Wendi Deng Murdoch, spent some US$150 million acquiring stakes in some twenty internet businesses across Asia. Buying at the very peak of the internet bubble, James's purchases ranged from Chinese sites like Netease and the Hong Kong-based Chinese-language portal renren.com, to a Bombay auction site and the Indian consumer portal Indya.com. Within a year, none of these investments would be worth a fraction of the value paid for them. Within two years all but a couple had disappeared completely.

James had also been the champion of News Corp's decision to merge its highly profitable *TV Guide* business with Gemstar International, run by Henry Yuen, a one-time maths professor whose patents put him at the forefront of the emerging business of creating onscreen program guides. Three years later, News Corp would take a US$6 billion write-down on its investment in Gemstar.

Still, despite a slightly spotted record, James, according to Murdoch senior, was the most suitable executive to take over the troubled STAR TV and migrate it from a basic pay-television plat-form to 'the leading multi-platform, multi-service digital media business in Asia'. The appointment of his son to the key Asian portfolio would also send a signal to the Beijing leadership that Murdoch retained a very real vested interest in his China opera-tions. Who better to have the ear of the world's leading media player than a son and heir? James had not been back to China since the first family visit there fifteen years earlier when, as a 10-year-old, he had accompanied his father on his inaugural visit to the Middle Kingdom. He had much to learn. But being the son of his father stood him in good stead, for the Chinese understood the dynamics of dynastic rule better than most. But it was an affray of almost Shakespearian proportions that the younger Murdoch walked into during his first months on the job, a feud between the scions of the enormously rich and powerful dynasties of the Lis and the Murdochs – Prince Richard vs Prince James.

Since Richard had out-manoeuvred the Murdochs earlier in the year in the takeover battle for Cable & Wireless HKT, he had also announced a new venture, Network of the World (NOW), which on paper at least, stood ready to go head to head with News Corp's satellite empire. Li's vision for NOW was a 'revolutionary new medium for the new generation of consumers in the digital age'. He promised to spend US$1.5 billion over five years developing interactive content for the new service, and had already built a slick studio in London with plans for three more, in Hong Kong, Tokyo and Bombay. In the months immediately after having lost the bid to wrestle control of HKT, the Murdochs tried to make the best of being good losers, with James on a number of occasions going out of his way to try to convince reporters that the proposed joint venture for STAR TV to provide programming content to HKT's fledgling broadband service could continue. He even dismissed as 'bullshit' suggestions that his father didn't have the best relationship with young Li. But by June the deal had collapsed.

In August, speaking at the Edinburgh International Television Festival in one of his first public speeches since taking the helm at STAR TV, James Murdoch took the simmering feud public. After months of insisting that there was no ill will between them, James let loose. He derided the interactive-broadcasting efforts of Li: 'I fail to understand how one can define a free-to-air English-language rehash of circa 1980 MTV as a global, multimedia, broadband, interactive TV service.'

Journalists who wrote favourable articles about Richard, the young Murdoch added, were afraid to point out the flaws in Li's business. Declared James: 'The emperor, I have to say, has no clothes on.' James took a further swipe at his rival's claims to having been the instigator of the STAR TV concept. 'When we bought the business, Richard Li had built a primarily English-language, analogue, five-channel, free-to-air distributor in the heart of Asia,' he said. 'Entirely an anathema to the broad diversity of the Asian so-called "marketplace".'

Richard Li responded a week later in a rebuke to his younger competitor that was widely circulated by the world's media.

'I won't comment,' he said. 'We'll wait until someone with a successful business track record makes comments and then we'll respond.

'We don't find it [James Murdoch's speech] very mature,' he said.

The following month, James took the opportunity to turn the tables on Richard Li's interactive broadband ambitions with a spoiling move in the potentially lucrative Taiwan market. The younger Murdoch had been assiduously courting Taiwan's powerful Koo family, whose GigaMedia corporation had previously signed up with Li's PCCW to roll out broadband interactive services across the island. However, in August the Koos announced an abrupt change of strategy, bailing out of the venture with PCCW. In September, GigaMedia announced it was partnering with STAR TV to provide interactive broadband television access using set-top boxes in a US$100 million joint venture. PCCW, on hearing of the deal, dismissed it as 'just another limited service', even though it had severely dented its own hopes of extending its interactive offerings beyond Hong Kong.

In hindsight it would have probably been better had James Murdoch kept his own counsel. Chinese culture dictates that rival dynastic heirs do not create a situation where either might incur a 'loss of face'. Criticism was strictly for behind closed doors and dirty linen was not aired in public. The young Murdoch's very public ragging of Richard Li was a sure indication that he had much to learn about doing business in China. Turning a business dispute into a personal clash and doing so on a stage before the world's media would not be seen as appropriate behaviour by the conservative Mandarins of the Beijing leadership, many of whom were on excellent terms with Li's father, the formidable Li Ka-shing. His comments on Richard Li's version of STAR TV being 'anathema' to the market's needs also cast doubts on his own father's strategy in Asia. It was, after all, Rupert Murdoch who had agreed to pay well above the odds to purchase STAR TV from the Li family.

Notionally, James Murdoch and Richard Li both saw the future in terms of a broadband interactive world. The recently announced merger between AOL and Time Warner had sent a shiver down the spine of even the most aggressive old media players. The deal seemingly represented the perfect industry model for a new media company. America Online had a large internet-access and subscription base. Time Warner controlled content – print, movies, TV, music – and a massive cable distribution system in the US. Whereas satellite was a great one-way delivery system for sending content to consumer, broadband cable allowed for two-way traffic. A relationship could be developed between the household and the operator. Whoever owned the set-top box inside the consumer's home owned the customer.

James Murdoch explained it to an interviewer thus: 'We call it the target wallet. The target wallet is going to get bigger as these markets grow. The share that we can capture gets bigger because the services have more breadth. Today, you pay X dollars for basic cable. Tomorrow, you will pay Y dollars for basic cable plus a premium tier with new channels and interactive services through a set-top box right in your house. That box is a relationship with the service operator. As the relationship gets tighter, it starts to do other things. It starts to be a "buy station" in the home. So the share of wallet [spent this way] grows into a wider share of overall household spending. We believe it is a natural evolution for media in this connected environment.'

In early 2000, STAR TV had only half the necessary elements of an interactive broadband platform in place. The company was transmitting TV programs to a potential 60 million viewers across Asia every day. However, STAR TV was only able to transmit and not receive – it desperately needed to strike a deal with the likes of GigaMedia to be able to successfully interface with its customers and take a percentage of every e-commerce deal that was done. PCCW, on the other hand, had just under 90 000 Hong Kong broadband subscribers through its HKT interactive TV network, plus about 840 000 dial-up subscribers. It also had little to show in the way of content apart from some Hollywood and Asian movies and the laughable offerings from its NOW studio in London.

Given the deep pockets available to the two rivals, it could have developed into a war of very significant proportions had it not been for the fact that the dot com bubble burst, numerically at least, on 10 March 2000, when the technology-heavy NASDAQ composite index peaked at 5048.62, more than double its value just a year before. The NASDAQ began to fall, slightly at first but with ever-increasing speed, dragging down the world's securities markets with it. On Monday, 13 March, investors, funds and institutions began to liquidate their dot com and tech stock holdings. In three days the NASDAQ lost nearly nine per cent, falling from roughly 5050 on 10 March to 4580 on 15 March. The dot coms were in full retreat, the worldwide broadband roll-out stalled to the point that there was suddenly an excess of capacity but no takers.

Over at PCCW, Richard Li was facing the daunting scenario of a share price that had fallen nearly 80 per cent since the highs that followed the acquisition of HKT and the announcement of his brave new world of broadband interactive entertainment heralded by the formation of NOW. Li was forced into making drastic cuts to his plans for NOW, folding it into the company's existing internet service in Hong Kong only and sacking some 340 of the NOW staff – 40 per cent of its workforce.

Rupert Murdoch and News Corp were also in retreat. The much vaunted spin-off of Sky Global had been deferred because of the decline in world stock market prices, NADP was being wound up, and every one of the company's internet properties around the world was having its budgets slashed and staff retrenched, or was simply closed down.

At the News Corp annual general meeting in Adelaide in October 2000, the elder Murdoch was even bragging that unlike his media rivals he had never really been taken in by the dot com revolution in the first place.

'We have not spent a fraction of what all our competitors have lost in this area,' he proclaimed proudly. 'We have slowed down and are slowing down. We have been very tentative and careful. In retrospect, we would have liked to have been even more so.'

It was also back to the drawing board for James Murdoch and STAR TV. His ambitious plans to create a 'multi-platform, multi-service media platform' in Asia – and China in particular – were on hold, although it didn't stop him pushing through an expensive re-branding campaign that was launched at year's end. The STAR TV Chairman and CEO wrote to senior industry professionals to explain that the company was dropping 'TV' from its brand identity. He said that the past ten years had seen a satellite broadcaster evolve into a company with strengths in content, distribution, radio and internet.

'By leveraging our brands, content, technology, local expertise and extensive infrastructure, and by forging important partnerships in key markets, we are actively creating the next generation of media connectivity in Asia. As STAR evolves from a television brand to a multi-service, multi-platform brand, we are evolving our identity from the media, i.e. from STAR TV, to the core of our brand, i.e. STAR.'

James also announced that STAR's new slogan would be 'Target Anyone, Anywhere'. And by 'anywhere' he was pretty much focusing on just two markets – China and India.

He began a series of regular visits to Beijing to acquaint himself with the authorities who presided over China's television affairs. James's strength was that despite his early stumbles in the new job, he was a keen listener who knew when it best served him to take advice from some of the more experienced managers around him. He began to lobby the SCIO and SARFT for News Corp to be allowed to open a production centre and sales office in Shanghai.

And STAR now needed sales in a big way. The idea of being able to tap into an e-commerce explosion that would follow the roll-out of broadband interactive television was now just a distant dream. James Murdoch would need to revert to the time-honoured tradition of advertising sales based around primetime popular viewing. He needed a ratings winner. He needed a *Judge Judy*.

16

Sons of the Patriarchs

A private dinner at Zhongnanhai, where China's Communist leaders live like royalty, marks perhaps the high point of Rupert Murdoch's adventures in China. His host, the General Secretary of the Chinese Communist Party and fifth President of the People's Republic of China, Jiang Zemin, sits at a large round table, facing the doorway with his back to the wall as dictated by Chinese protocol. Immediately to Jiang's right, in the seat of honour, sits Murdoch, while on the President's left, Mrs Wendi Deng Murdoch parlays with Ding Guangen, the powerful former nemesis of Murdoch who now greets his guests with effusive warmth.

Opposite Jiang, on the other side of the table, sits James Murdoch, beaming broadly after being introduced to the President by his father as his new personal full-time envoy to China and the Chairman and Chief Executive of STAR. Also at the table sit another two senior Chinese government ministers and two senior

News Corporation executives. It's a rare and extraordinary honour for any Western business leader to be afforded a private dinner inside the Beijing leadership compound – even more so that the Murdoch family should be present. It was 5 January 2001 and by now the relationship between the leader of the upcoming world superpower and arguably the world's most powerful media tycoon had reached the *lao pengyou* or 'old friend' stage, where discussions were far more open and wide-ranging than the formal East–West tone which had prevailed previously. Indeed there was a good deal of laughter and mirth around the table, where Western-style pepper steaks were being served.

Not discussed, at least overtly, was a further cementing of bonds between the two powerful patriarchs. Earlier, the elder Murdoch has signed off on a deal to invest some US$60 million in China Netcom, a company backed and chaired by the Chinese President's son, Jiang Mianheng. China Netcom, at the time an 18-month-old firm based in Beijing backed by powerful government departments such as the Ministry of Railways and SARFT, was building a 5300-mile fibre optic network linking 50 million people in seventeen of China's most prosperous cities. Its broadband network was a direct challenge to one being built by China Telecom, the country's former telephone monopoly, and was widely being touted as the largest and most advanced in China. However, China Netcom needed to raise an additional US$327 million to fund the continued roll-out of network and had persuaded

Murdoch, along with other foreign investors including Goldman Sachs, Dell Computer's founder Michael Dell and Kerry Group's Robert Kuok, to kick in the necessary funds. At the time of the Zhongnanhai dinner, Murdoch's investment was still technically illegal as Chinese law forbade foreign investment in the telecoms sector. Nevertheless, Jiang Mianheng had been able to assure his new foreign partners it would only be a matter of time before China Netcom would be able to use its connections to obtain a special dispensation to allow the fundraising to proceed. In the meantime, the deal needed to remain secret.

The deal had in fact been negotiated over months in meetings between the younger Jiang and the younger Murdoch, along with Wendi Deng and the CEO of China Netcom, Edward Tian. Wendi, Tian and Jiang Mianheng enjoyed a common bond – they had all been educated in the US and had returned to make their fortunes in China, by one means or another.

Jiang Mianheng had left China in 1986 to get his doctorate in high-temperature superconductivity from Drexel University in Philadelphia, before moving to Silicon Valley in 1991 to take up a position with Hewlett Packard developing its business strategy for Asia. In 1992 he returned home and joined the Shanghai Institute of Metallurgy, where he spun off a manufacturing company from the state agency. The company, Simtek, became a highly profitable manufacturer of mobile phone components for foreign corporations such as Ericsson. In 1999 Jiang junior was credited with convincing his father's inner circle to approve a new company that would break the monopoly of the state-owned telecommunication companies. China Netcom launched in November 1999.

In March 2000, a Jiang-backed networking company, AsiaInfo Holdings, founded by Edward Tian, soared 315 per cent in its first day of trading on the NASDAQ largely as a result of its perceived China connections. Tian had returned to China in 1991 following his US education and began providing key internet software and systems to the Chinese telecoms and banking sectors. After the successful float of AsiaInfo, he was tapped to become the CEO of China Netcom.

Yale MBA Wendi Deng developed a good rapport with her fellow American-educated alumni Jiang Mianheng and Tian. Wendi introduced her stepson James to the pair and an ongoing dialogue had followed. The China Netcom deal was a very significant victory for News Corp, given that Jiang Mianheng had also been avidly courted by Viacom's Sumner Redstone and AOL Time Warner's Jerry Levin in the preceding year. So it was a shock to all when the news of the China Netcom deal was finally made public a month after the Zhongnanhai dinner. Not only had News Corp been able to seemingly circumvent Chinese law, but Rupert Murdoch had been named a director of China Netcom. Murdoch was on a roll.

But if China Netcom was not a topic of conversation during the dinner with President Jiang, then the Murdoch collective present had another agenda. They wanted Jiang's support for a high-profile media summit to be held in Shanghai during the coming October, to coincide with the 2001 APEC Leaders Meeting. The summit, to be sponsored by News Corp and hopefully attended by the world's leading media executives, was being promoted by the Murdochs as a means of showcasing China's opening to the outside world and building 'mutual understanding and cooperation' with the international media. In reality, the idea was to use the proposed summit as a means of bolstering News Corp in China – particularly STAR's brand – while gaining valuable kudos as a great supporter of the Chinese people. Rupert Murdoch also saw it as a means of countering what he saw as the growing influence of his rival, Jerry Levin, whose Fortune Global Forum in Hong Kong during the coming May would again feature Jiang Zemin as its keynote speaker.

The AOL Time Warner merger would be announced within a few days of Murdoch's Beijing visit on 10 January. The deal, basically AOL acquiring Time Warner Inc. for US$182 billion in stock and debt, would create a digital media powerhouse. Murdoch was also aware that Levin was the only media mogul who enjoyed a personal relationship with Jiang Zemin equal or better to his own. The Fortune Global Forum in Shanghai in 1999 had provided Levin and Time Warner with enormous standing amongst the Beijing leadership and the 2001 event in Hong Kong looked likely to repeat its success. As far as the ingratiation stakes went, Murdoch was not going to be outdone in what he now regarded as his own backyard.

Jiang gave Murdoch the nod for his proposed media summit. Dinner finished with a great deal of mutual backslapping and vigorous handshaking. The official News Corp party retired to the Long March Bar of Beijing's exclusive China Club to congratulate themselves on the results of the evening's efforts. Jiang Zemin and his offsiders may have likewise been having a celebratory glass of something. After all, they had just engineered a play-off between the world's two most powerful and influential media companies to see which could do a better job of promoting the interests of China to the outside world.

In February AOL Time Warner made a further move into what had hitherto been virtually Murdoch's exclusive territory with the re-launch of the China Entertainment Television satellite channel (CETV) into China. The company had acquired a majority stake in CETV from its founders and owners, the former Hong Kong media personalities Robert and Peggy Chua, who had actually managed to get a toe-hold in the China market with their 'no sex, no violence, no news' style of programming but who lacked the *guanxi* and financial resources to make it commercially viable. CETV was re-launched as an 'infotainment' channel, offering some original programming plus re-runs of the popular Japanese children's animated series *Powerpuff Girls* and dubbed action programs. The channel itself was poorly funded by AOL Time Warner and compared to Murdoch's joint venture Phoenix Channel it ran a distant and fairly dismal second.

But the arrival of CETV spurred Murdoch into action. It was not just that CETV represented competition in the marketplace, but that STAR didn't have its 'own' channel in China. The Phoenix Chinese Channel was in fact doing very well – its advertising revenue was exceeding that of STAR's other channels combined, and Murdoch's joint venture partner Liu Changle had recently launched Phoenix Infonews, a 24-hour Chinese-language news and information channel that was being critically well received by those up-market Chinese viewers able to access the signal. But Murdoch was never happy with the Phoenix arrangement, which gave him neither majority ownership nor editorial control. As part of the original Phoenix deal STAR had agreed to pull its own Chinese-language entertainment channel from its platform offering. Now that AOL Time Warner had launched CETV, Murdoch wanted that agreement overturned. He wanted his own channel, even if it meant going head-to-head with Phoenix and competing for the same advertising dollars.

But advertising dollars were still hard to come by as each of the three Chinese entertainment channels was officially limited to top hotels and official compounds. While the advertising sales-men could justifiably claim millions of unofficial viewers watching pirated signals, the advertisers themselves wanted some semblance of 'landing rights' or official carriage having been granted by Beijing to the satellite channel operators. STAR, Phoenix and AOL Time Warner all needed legal access to the Chinese cable systems if they were to ever recoup the cost of their investments. So began an extraordinary lobbying campaign by all parties concerned of the SCIO, of the Propaganda Department and of Jiang himself. Ding Guangen couldn't believe his luck.

Certainly James Murdoch wasted no time in trying to curry favour with the Chinese leadership and define his credentials as his father's man in China. In late March, speaking at the Milken Institute's annual business conference in Beverly Hills, James startled his audience with a zealous defence of Beijing's harsh crackdown on Falun Gong and criticism of Hong Kong democracy supporters. He referred to the Falun Gong spiritual movement as 'dangerous' and an 'apocalyptic cult' and went on to lambast the Western press for its negative portrayal of the giant Asian nation.

Falun Gong, also known as Falun Dafa, is a spiritual movement that combines meditation and exercise and was banned by the Chinese government after 10 000 followers staged a protest in Tiananmen Square in 1999. Its banning had more to do with its ability to organise mass demonstrations than its political or other beliefs, in a country where the Communist Party still liked to think it had complete control. At the time of the younger Murdoch's comments even the US State Department was claiming that Chinese authorities jailed thousands of Falun Gong practitioners and at least 100 had died in prison as a result of neglect or torture. The crackdown on Falun Gong, which had been ordered by Jiang Zemin, was being orchestrated by the same officials who had once been given the task of monitoring and controlling Rupert Murdoch's entry into China – Public Security head Luo Gan and the Propaganda Department's Ding Guangen, now a firm friend of the Murdoch family.

As his father watched from the audience, James claimed that Falun Gong 'clearly does not have the success of China at heart' and accused the Western media of 'painting a falsely negative portrayal of China through their focus on controversial issues such as human rights and Taiwan'. Even the democracy advocates in James's new home town of Hong Kong came in for criticism, with the media heir suggesting that they 'accept the reality of life' under a strong-willed, 'absolutist' government.

A chip off the old block, perhaps. But coming from the son of a father who presented himself as a champion of the free market conservative right, James's comments caused a good deal of indignation around the traps. Even the normally pro-business, conservative *Wall Street Journal* let rip with an opinion piece written by its deputy features editor Tunku Varadarajan, who labelled Rupert 'a master practitioner of the corporate kowtow' for instructing James, 'a college dropout', in the 'craft of craven submission to the Communist regime in China'. Needless to say, there was no apology or clarification from the Murdochs regarding reports of James's speech, which received a good run in the media back in mainland China.

Two months later, members of Falun Gong, whose protests

had always been peaceful, were singled out for special treatment prior to the AOL Time Warner-sponsored Fortune Global Forum conference in Hong Kong. In May, about 100 members of the group were detained and then deported by immigration officials at the Hong Kong airport for no apparent reason. During the conference, those Falun Gong members who intended to protest the imprisonment and torture of the sect's followers in China were moved by police to areas well beyond the forum venue, in order that President Jiang be spared hearing their dissenting voices. Even as AOL Time Warner officials negotiated in the background of the meeting with their Chinese counterparts to have a ban on *Time* magazine in China (for having published a story on Falun Gong) lifted, Jerry Levin was welcoming Jiang Zemin to the stage of the Fortune Global Forum, referring to the President as a 'good friend', and declaring him 'a man of honour dedicated to the best interests of his people'. It was mild compared to James Murdoch's clumsy ingratiation in Los Angeles, but designed nonetheless to let Jiang and his entourage know that AOL Time Warner were also trusted friends of the Beijing leadership.

The following month, Jerry Levin was back in Beijing to sign a US$200 million deal between AOL Time Warner and China's largest computer maker, Legend Computers. The venture planned to offer broadband internet access to customers in mainland China through AOL software installed in Legend computers. Coming as it did just months after the public announcement of Murdoch's

China Netcom deal, Levin appeared to be matching his News Corp rival step-for-step across China.

By mid-2001 Murdoch had also finalised his plans for STAR's own Chinese-language entertainment channel, to be known as Xing Kong Wei Shi, or 'Starry Sky'. The new channel would be vying for viewers from both CETV and his own joint venture Phoenix channel – an outcome that would be a source of considerable ongoing friction with partner Liu Changle. But the commercial viability of each channel was still dependent upon being granted landing rights in China. It was a matter of going cap-in-hand to Beijing in a veritable beauty parade of who could offer what in return for carriage on China's rapidly expanding cable television networks. Officially, News Corp and AOL Time Warner were to deal through CCTV's commercial subsidiary, China International Television Corporation (CITVC), which was charged with developing China's television media industry. In reality, any decision would be made by Ding Guangen and the SCIO.

It was a situation perfectly suited to the Chinese, who had become masters at playing off over-eager Western multinationals enthralled by the prospect of entering the potentially lucrative China market. During the 1980s and early 1990s Beijing was able to successfully manoeuvre the world's biggest oil companies into a bidding war against each other. By the mid-1990s the Chinese authorities had convinced upwards of fifty Western oil companies to accept all of the costs of conducting seismic exploration in the South China and Yellow seas, interpreting their data and drawing up exploitation plans, before making all the information available to the Chinese, on the basis that in the future they might be entitled to bid for plots to do exploratory drilling on terms as yet undecided by China. It made little economic sense on the part of the Western oil companies, but they were all so entranced by the lure of the market that it seemed a small price to pay to be first in the door.

Now, with some of the world's biggest media players knocking on its door, the SCIO saw its chance to take full advantage of a bidding war. Part of the Propaganda Department's role, and therefore that of the SCIO, was to propagate a 'positive and accurate picture' of China to the outside world. To this end, the SCIO had been a driving force behind the creation of CCTV 9, a 24-hour English news and information channel that was launched on 25 September 2000. CCTV 9 was intended to present a Chinese perspective on events and issues within China and abroad, and provide an alternative to news about China from sources such as CNN, APTN and Reuters, who up to that point supplied the bulk of images from China seen internationally.

But having created a means for China to present its own side of the nation's story, the Chinese authorities needed to try to ensure that the outside world had the opportunity to view it. Previously, while the service was being made available via satellite to some parts of the world, the SCIO had experienced little success in convincing key overseas cable and satellite operators that they should carry the channel as part of their platform offering. Most operators saw it as little more than a mouthpiece for the Chinese government. The SCIO also claimed that it was not in a position to pay Western media platform operators to carry the channel. Consequently, CCTV 9 was hardly seen outside of China itself – that was, until Rupert and Jerry walked in the door.

The SCIO now had a simple proposition for both News Corp and AOL Time Warner – reciprocal carriage. It was a non-negotiable offer. The Western media companies could have access to China's cable system so long as they made CCTV 9 available on their cable and satellite systems in the West. More specifically, the SCIO was offering restricted carriage on a cable television system in Guangdong province in return for CCTV 9 carriage on the key Time Warner cable network in New York and Washington, and the Fox Cable systems in Los Angeles and San Francisco, as well as on the BSkyB platform in Europe. It was a no-cost option for the SCIO, but not so for the Western media giants, who would either have to bump an existing paying customer from their platforms to make way for CCTV 9 or forego revenue from a channel that might otherwise be available for lease.

In return, the SCIO was offering access to about 600 000 subscribers on the Guangdong Cable Television network in southern China. The downside was that they were all Mandarin-language services, and Guangdong was a predominantly Cantonese-speaking province in the Pearl River Delta that was already well-served by Hong Kong's Cantonese-speaking media. They would thus be attempting to push Mandarin-language television in a province where the two Hong Kong channels commanded nearly 60 per cent of viewing time. In pure economic terms it was far from a great deal, but like the oil companies before them, both sides took the bait in the rush to be first to market.

On 19 October 2001 James Murdoch proudly announced to the world that 'China had opened its television market to News Corporation's Phoenix Chinese channel', allowing it to broadcast into the Pearl River Delta. 'As a major shareholder of Phoenix, STAR is very pleased about this development. We see it as yet another milestone for Phoenix,' he proclaimed. What was left unsaid was the fact that News Corp had agreed to provide CCTV9 with a channel on its new BSkyB platform in the UK.

Four days later, AOL Time Warner announced what it termed a 'Historic Reciprocal Cable TV Carriage Agreement With China', claiming that the deal meant that CETV would be the first foreign TV channel to be granted cable carriage rights in China. Jerry Levin was absolutely gushing in trumpeting the deal:

We are very pleased to have achieved this landmark agreement, which represents a significant step in the growing relation-ship between AOL Time Warner and the people of China. It is part of a sustained effort by our operating divisions to work with Chinese partners in creating products and services for this dynamic marketplace. Today's agreement provides us further opportunities to collaborate with local talent and to continue the mutually beneficial exchange of knowledge and expertise. The reciprocal nature of the agreement means that American audiences will gain a greater understanding of Chinese culture as well as an appreciation for the immense intellect, artistry and creativity of the Chinese people.

Levin at least acknowledged that it was a 'reciprocal deal', unlike News Corp, but both companies opted to put the best spin possible on the story and failed to mention they were launching Mandarin channels into predominantly Cantonese-speaking markets.

On 19 December, James Murdoch announced News Corp's version of a 'historic agreement' – this time it was the permission of the Chinese authorities to allow STAR to launch its new Chinese-language entertainment channel, Xing Kong Wei Shi, which would also be allowed to access the Guangdong Cable Television network. Like the previously announced Phoenix deal, this too, according to James Murdoch, 'marked a milestone of STAR's development in China'. And like the other 'historic' deals and 'milestones' in China's television industry, this one was also predicated on News Corp's Fox cable network carrying CCTV 9 on the US West Coast.

Present at the Xing Kong announcement in Beijing was Ding

Guangen, who remarked that 'the agreement marks a good beginning of the cooperation between the two parties, which will be gradually expanded'.

If anyone should have been in the Long March Bar at the China Club that evening buying drinks, it should have been Ding Guangen. He had successfully played off two of the world's biggest media companies, had their chief executives fawning over the Chinese President, and now, for no cost, had established CCTV 9 – the new voice of China – on both the US West and East Coasts, and in the heart of the United Kingdom and Europe.

Ding Guangen was on a roll.

17

Reality Bites

The thing about Rupert Murdoch is that he backs his judgment. He is always prepared to put his money – or at least his shareholders' money – where his mouth is. With the launch of the Mandarin channel Xing Kong Wei Shi in March 2002, two of the world's largest and most influential media companies – News Corporation and AOL Time Warner – were going head-to-head to grab a stake in the potentially lucrative China market. But whereas AOL Time Warner was hoping for a breakthrough for its recently acquired CETV channel with a programming schedule of dubbed Western action shows and cartoon classics from its existing library, Murdoch announced Xing Kong would be commissioning nearly 700 hours of original, locally produced material. Whereas AOL Time Warner was backing reruns of *Tom and Jerry*, Murdoch was putting his bets on *Judge Judy*, or at least a Chinese version of it.

Murdoch, or more particularly younger son James in his role as Chairman and Chief Executive of STAR, had decreed that what China's television viewers needed was a diet of localised, lightweight, mass-appeal programming similar to that which had helped News Corp's Fox Television reach the top of the network ratings in the US. James was telling News Corp's investors that while STAR had serious problems with distribution in China, the solution was about 'programming'. He was promulgating a 'build it and they will come' scenario in which he argued that China, in reality, was no different from any other market – the key was to provide compulsive programming. Produce 'something that every-one wants to watch, and you are pretty sure that you are going to get distribution cracked at some time', was how he explained it to the STAR staff.

One of the first incarnations of James's programming for the Chinese masses was *TV Court*, a knock-off of the popular Ameri-can reality courtroom series *Judge Judy* with its tough-talking, no-nonsense, real-life courtroom drama. But instead of a middle-aged, retired Family Court judge, the Xing Kong version opted for an attractive twenty-something court official in re-enactments of what were supposed to be real-life Beijing court cases. It would have been interesting to observe the reactions of some of Beijing's dour conservative leadership to one of the first episodes broadcast in which the defendant, a Beijing resident, was being held accountable for keeping a pet donkey in his apartment. His neighbour, perhaps justifiably, was arguing that in a city where even the keeping of pet dogs was strictly limited according to their size, the keeping of farm animals was illegal. The defendant's response was that his donkey had never lived on a farm and therefore was not a farm animal, nor could it be classified under the dog ordinance. Naturally the judge, doing the right thing not to antagonise Chinese censors, ordered the donkey out of the apartment.

Certainly, Murdoch has never been afraid to rock the establishment. But the advent of the likes of *Judge Judy* in China needs to be seen against the sort of programs viewers were getting from the state-owned public broadcasting behemoth, CCTV. In 2002, the same year that STAR was embarking on its campaign of churning out voyeuristic reality show fare, the highlights of the CCTV production calendar were *The Clarion Army Song*, a twenty-part drama reflecting the 'developmental history of the Chinese army', *The Making of New China, Mao Zedong in 1925*, and *Long March*, described as a 'panorama of the Red Army's heroic conducts and activities during the Long March, like conquering the snow-capped mountains and wading through the wetlands, by traversing along the road the Red Army actually crossed'.

Under James' watchful eye, STAR had opened a new office in Shanghai and appointed an up-and-coming, ambitious young American executive, Jamie Davis, as President of STAR China to oversee its localisation efforts. Davis had joined News Corp from CBS Sports, taking a position with Fox Sports in the US before coming to Hong Kong as CFO of STAR Sports. He formed a close bond with James and was soon after appointed Senior Vice President, overseeing the broadcaster's movie and general entertainment channels before being tapped to head the China operation. It seemed to matter little to the Murdochs that Davis had no previous China experience, nor that he spoke neither Mandarin nor Cantonese at the time. What he lacked in experience, he made up for in unbridled energy and enthusiasm.

Davis spearheaded a multitude of deals with China's leading television production companies to produce the necessary material for Xing Kong's new programming schedule. By the start of 2003, the STAR line-up under Davis's tutelage included such titles as *Woman in Control*, a beauty contest for men; *Love Factory*, in which a bevy of Chinese personalities provided matchmaking advice; and *Battle of the Cooking Gods*, based on the Japanese *Iron Chef* series, which pitted chefs from across China in a competition blending sport and cooking.

Other highlights included the dance contest show *Live! From Xing Kong Dance Club* and the *Xing Kong Cave* quiz show, set inside a surreal cave where contestants were held upside down and dropped several metres onto a cushioned floor below if they answered a series of questions incorrectly. Other knock-offs from the Fox Network successful US programming schedule included a local take on *America's Most Wanted* called *Wanted! In China*, which involved re-enacting grisly mainland murders, and a talk show with a wisecracking host in the vein of the *Tonight Show with Jay Leno*, called *Late Night Talk*.

That News Corp was able to produce some 700 hours of original programming in just over a year was no mean feat given that foreign production companies were not allowed to independently produce television shows in China. They had to commission local partners to do it for them while ensuring a level of quality was maintained. In addition, every episode of every show had to be pre-approved by censors from the Propaganda Department. Documents that had to be produced before the censors gave the go-ahead for any production included a letter of application; a summary in Chinese of at least 1500 words per episode; résumés of producers, directors and scriptwriters; a list of actors, actresses and other staff; a production plan; shooting locations and detailed filming schedule; a memorandum on joint production; investment certification; and a production permit from the Chinese partner.

But, even then, Davis and STAR sometimes pushed the limits of China's newfound tolerance just too far. One of its first and most vaunted proposals was for a situation comedy to be modelled on the American hit *Friends*. STAR signed an agreement with the Beijing-based Yings Productions for a forty-episode series to be called *Joyful Youth*, 'about three young single women who share an apartment – their passions in life and the hilarious situations they fall into'. Unfortunately, during the review process the SARFT censors objected to a scene in which a male character

made derisive comments about the small size of a female neighbour's breasts. After a further review of the submitted scripts
the censors decided that a public dissemination of the lives of
three young Chinese women was not in the interests of Chinese
cultural purity, and they refused to issue a series permit – this
despite Xing Kong having already previewed the first few episodes.
The SARFT censors demanded STAR pull *Joyful Youth* from its
programming schedule forthwith.

By this time I was back in Hong Kong working for the AOL
Time Warner subsidiary CNN International, as Managing Editor
in the Asia Pacific. But because of my previous China experience
with News Corp, I was also a member of the AOL Time Warner
Greater China Council – a committee made up of representatives
of the company's various operations with the aim of achieving
some sort of coordination in relation to existing or planned activities in China. At this early stage of the completed merger between
the dial-up service and the traditional media company, AOL
still saw itself as very much the senior partner in the relationship and its representatives swaggered about with a great deal
of arrogance. AOL was in the midst of the proposed US$200
million cooperative deal with Legend Computers. Warner Bros
was about to invest millions in building and operating a chain
of multiplex cinemas. Turner Broadcasting Systems (TBS Asia
Pacific) had been given the task of overseeing the operations
of the fledgling CETV Chinese-language channel as it went to

battle with Murdoch's Xing Kong Wei Shi.

It was a 'no-contest' from round one. The Murdoch juggernaut simply out-spent, out-muscled and outshone its CETV rival. TBS had allocated some US$17 million to fund the CETV operation. For that it was producing less than 20 per cent original programming – largely studio-based chat shows and re-hashed news reports – with the rest of the programming schedule being made up of dubbed action series from the Time Warner library or dubbed imports from South Korea, Taiwan and Japan. The AOL Time Warner board was simply not prepared to risk any more of its shareholders' funds in a market that still offered only limited 'official' penetration to Western broadcasters. Murdoch, on the other hand, had no such qualms. By the estimates of those on the AOL Time Warner Greater China Council, STAR had to be spending in excess of US$60 million during the start-up phase of Xing Kong. It was widely trumpeting the fact that the new channel would achieve in excess of 60 per cent local programming within one year of launching.

At one of the AOL Time Warner China Council meetings in early 2003 there was a discussion about an article in *Time* magazine (another Time Warner subsidiary) which covered the Xing Kong phenomenon. It quoted STAR's Jamie Davis as saying: 'We wanted programming like they'd never seen. We wanted that international format and energy. But you have to go local to succeed.'

We understood that much. What we could not comprehend

was how News Corp could justify the spending on the new channel which, officially, was still confined to three-star hotels and above, international and official compounds and one cable system in the predominantly Cantonese-speaking province of Guangdong. CETV was burning through nearly US$1.5 million a month in expenses, and advertising revenues barely topped US$40 000 in the same period. It was a pretty difficult case to argue to head office that CETV needed more funds to match the Murdoch competition.

But the STAR strategy was predicated on Murdoch's absolute belief that his now well-established relationship with President Jiang Zemin and his 'old friends' in the Propaganda Department would soon deliver much more than Guangdong province. He was convinced China would open up its broadcast cable networks and that News Corp would be well positioned to roll out Xing Kong across the country. Davis said as much in his interview with *Time*.

'In the long run, yes, I want to be national,' he said. 'I wouldn't put in this kind of money if I thought that twenty-five years from now I'm still going to be in Guangdong province.'

Murdoch had to expand beyond Guangdong to justify the enormous investment he was making. He believed that Beijing's approval of landing rights for Xing Kong in the province was merely a test to see whether News Corp could provide programming that stayed within the government-imposed confines of what constituted acceptable content. Those confines prohibited the broadcast of material that was deemed harmful to national unity, sovereignty or territorial integrity; was harmful to national security, honour or interest; incited ethnic division or damaged ethnic unity; revealed state secrets; defamed or insulted other persons; or contained obscene, superstitious or excessively violent material, or other content prohibited by laws and administrative statutes.

With the possible exception of *Joyful Youth*, STAR had managed to satisfy the censors from at least the security point of view. But if Murdoch thought that the Beijing leadership was about to hand him the keys to China's lounge rooms, then he wasn't reading either the tea-leaves or the Chinese media correctly.

What was concerning to every media company seeking access to the China market were reports emanating from the official Chinese media that the authorities had no intention of allowing any expansion of landing rights beyond Guangdong. In March 2003 the Chinese media was quoting CCTV Vice President Zhang Changming as saying that the CETV and Xing Kong Wei Shi channels were not likely to be permitted to extend their services beyond the Pearl River Delta region in the near future.

'After all, the TV business is about ideology and propaganda,' he added. 'For us, social responsibility is more important [than entertainment].'

If Zhang was throwing cold water on STAR's advance, then James Murdoch refused to be deterred. A similar mix of popular reality programming in India was paying big dividends for the broadcaster's operations there. STAR's localised Indian version of *Who Wants to Be a Millionaire,* known in Hindi as *Kaun Banega Crorepati*, shattered ratings records and spawned several copycat game shows. A mixture of more game shows based on successful US productions, followed by new locally produced Hindi drama series, helped catapult STAR from being an also-ran to the number one cable service in India. STAR's success had in fact started to shift the company's centre of gravity from China to India as James saw the opportunity for far healthier returns in the South Asian advertising markets than in those of elusive North Asia.

Nonetheless, with his father's ongoing backing, James continued to pour money into developing Xing Kong. The new channel was voted 'Satellite Channel of the Year' at the 2002 China Television Program Awards and STAR press releases were touting it as the 'highest-rating regional Mandarin-language satellite channel in Guangdong'. Such a statement was akin to announcing that CCTV 9 was the highest-rating international television channel in New York – there was not a lot of competition. At AOL Time Warner, by our estimates, of the twenty-odd television channels available to most Guangdong homes, Xing Kong rated fourteenth and CETV twentieth. Not such a great return on the investment to date.

STAR needed distribution beyond what had been 'officially' defined by the authorities. Some of the more unscrupulous cable operators simply down-linked Xing Kong's most popular shows, removed the STAR advertising slots and inserted their own before re-broadcasting the programs on their own channels. But the real consequence of Murdoch's downmarket, populist approach was to unleash a wave of copycat or cloned programming, which effectively moved the entire Chinese broadcast market into a new era of lowbrow reality and infotainment television. Anywhere else, Murdoch could have tapped a potential goldmine, but in China, where there was little respect for copyright and virtually no enforcement of what rules there were, Xing Kong opened the doors to the competition. And the competition was subject to none of the restrictive shackles that had been imposed on foreign broadcasters to date.

Although CCTV was the only truly national broadcaster, there were around 600 other terrestrial broadcasters in China by 2003. An example of the Chinese ability to clone successful programming formats was the oft-cited case of the popular Taiwan dating show *Special Man and Woman*. The show featured a group of young people set a series of tasks culminating in a match-off of couples, but also involved audience participation featuring family members, friends and workmates barracking and influencing the judging. The show was originally aired on Murdoch's joint venture Phoenix Chinese Channel in 1997. Within a year the show was then emulated by one of the more radical and successful Chinese television operations, Hunan Satellite Television, and launched as

Romantic Meeting. Over the course of the next two years it turned up in various guises, including on Beijing Cable TV as *Everlasting Romance*, on Shanghai Television as *Saturday Meeting*, on Beijing Television as *Tonight We Become Acquainted*, on Nanjing Cable TV as *Conjugal Bliss*, on Hebei Television as *The Square of Kindred Spirits*, on Nanjing TV as *Who Does Your Heart Beat For?*, on Shanxi TV as *Good Man, Good Woman*, and so on and so on. By the end of 2003 there were reckoned to be some 200 versions of the show being broadcast across China.

Even the previously staid CCTV entered the fray – first with its own take on *Who Wants to Be a Millionaire*, re-titled *Happy Dictionary*, in which contestants could win cash by answering questions about science, history and current events. CCTV also co-produced the first knock-off of *Survivor* in China, entitled *Journey to Shangri-La*, which involved a thirty-day trek across the fringes of the Himalayas by three teams of six people with ten days' supply of matches and food. When the national broadcaster advertised for potential contestants, it received more than 200 000 applicants.

The Murdochs' strategy was to try buy market share by throwing money at localised programming at such a rate that it surely could never be matched by his Chinese counterparts. But they underestimated how quick the Chinese were at cloning anything that looked like a successful format and just how deep were their pockets. Imitations of a score of innovative game show programs appeared on rival cable channels, often within weeks of the show premiering on Xing Kong.

Over at AOL Time Warner, meantime, the debate was whether or not to program a dubbed Mandarin-language version of the US socio-political drama series *The West Wing* to cable homes in Cantonese-speaking Guangdong. There appeared to be no great rush by the Chinese television industry to emulate *that* show.

In 2003 the Chinese government's official figures put the value of the country's television advertising spend at around US$3.1 billion. There were already close to 100 million homes with cable television across the nation, each capable of receiving at least twenty channels. Even so, AOL Time Warner's conservative approach was failing to make the slightest of dents in these markets. By the end of 2003 it had spent some US$40 million on the acquisition and operational costs of CETV and in that financial year reported a loss of around US$17 million on revenues of just US$450 000.

At STAR, James Murdoch was telling a different story, based on the success of his programming fare of reality TV and lowbrow drama. As a result, the company had recorded its first full-year profit – some US$10 million based on revenues of around US$300 million – although it was widely thought that India accounted for up to 90 per cent of those advertising sales. Still, it was a marked turnaround on the US$100 million losses of three years earlier and STAR China President Jamie Davis was claiming that his turnover was up 180 per cent and predicting that the China operation would be profitable in its own right by the end of 2005. Or, at least, it would be providing Rupert Murdoch's Beijing connections played ball and allowed STAR to expand its distribution beyond the restricted realms of Cantonese-speaking Guangdong.

But the winds of change were blowing in Beijing and Rupert Murdoch, normally so adept at sniffing the political breeze in Western political enclaves of Washington, London and Canberra, had failed to pick up on the scent.

18

Changing of the Guard

One would have thought there was about as much chance of US President George W Bush attending an al-Qaeda fund-raiser as there was of Rupert Murdoch being invited to speak to the prestigious Party School of the China Communist Party Central Committee in downtown Beijing. The Central Party School is the main think-tank of China's highest policy-making body, the Politburo Standing Committee, and exists to indoctrinate the country's highest-level officials in the interpretation of communist ideology.

Murdoch, on the other hand, had long been considered a high priest of Western capitalism. No tycoon had been more aggressive or more successful in expanding an empire across multinational boundaries, nor more prepared to parlay media power in return for political influence in the democracies of the US, Britain and Australia. Murdoch's outspoken support for free markets unfettered by state regulation and government interference would seem to sit uncomfortably with the Chinese leadership's views on a controlled economy and support for the proletariat. But here he was, on 8 October 2003, stepping up to the lectern to deliver a lecture to the elite cadres of the China Communist Party.

Murdoch had been invited to speak to the Party School by its Principal, Zeng Qinghong, concurrently Vice President of China and a protégé of the former Chinese leader Jiang Zemin. The position of Party School Principal is one of great prestige within the CCP hierarchy. It had previously been occupied by the new Chinese President, Hu Jintao, who had been able to exert very significant influence over Party thinking during his term as Principal. Zeng, considered by many observers to have been a rival to Hu for the top job, and Jiang's preferred successor, had been in the role just six months when he controversially invited Murdoch, a man considered by many of the CCP's conservative elders to be the 'ultimate capitalist roader', to address the school's graduating class of ministerial and provincial-level party officials.

But as controversial as Murdoch was, there were many in the Chinese leadership who felt they understood him and could work with him. He was, after all, an 'emperor' in their own mould. I had lost count of the number of times Chinese officials had asked me to draw a diagram of the News Corp management structure. I would respond by drawing a small circle surrounded by an increasing number of larger concentric circles. 'Murdoch is like the Sun King,' I would explain. 'He is at the centre and his businesses and executive revolve around him.' The Chinese officials would nod approvingly. This was akin to the Chinese emperors of old who operated with the 'mandate of heaven' and whose word was law. Even Murdoch's dynastic tendencies of placing his children in key executive positions, to ensure they were well-placed to step in and run the empire after his demise, was well-accepted by a ruling elite for whom nepotism was a widely established practice. Murdoch's was a management structure they admired and understood. It was a far cry from the myriad of chief executives who came knocking on their door promising all manner of things only to fail, citing excuses of having to defer to boards of directors or shareholders' wishes. Murdoch, by contrast, made decisions on the spot and followed through. His was a model to the Chinese leadership's liking.

In the audience during Murdoch's speech to the assembled Party School cadres was Zeng himself, along with a number of Cabinet Ministers and senior Communist Party officials. James Murdoch was also there to hear his father give the gathering of future communist leaders the benefit of his thoughts on the economy and the media. There was a certain irony in the fact that the speech in which Murdoch now extolled the prospects of China's media was taking place nearly ten years to the day since the Beijing leadership had signed into law State Council Proclamation No. 129 banning the purchase or possession of satellite dishes by ordinary Chinese, in response to the tycoon's famous declaration that 'satellite technology was an unambiguous threat to totalitarian regimes everywhere'.

But now a decade on, and having proven his loyalty and support for China's cause, Murdoch was no longer making threatening noises. Instead he was talking up the Chinese media industry, encouraging his audience to 'let it [the media] flourish'.

'The potential of the open market doesn't represent any loss of power,' he said. 'China has the potential not only to follow the examples of the US and the UK, but to improve upon those examples and achieve a level of success all its own.

'By developing a regulatory system that is both firm enough to ensure China's control over her emerging businesses and smart enough not to stifle those businesses' growth, China will create an exemplary media industry.'

There was warm applause from the audience for its guest speaker at the end of his dissertation, in which he was basically saying that News Corp would accept Chinese regulation and editorial control so long as it didn't get in the way of the company making money. In typical fashion, Murdoch had not wasted the opportunity to push his own barrow, a point picked up by some of the more sceptical listeners in the audience. A week later a critique of Murdoch's lecture by Professor Yu Guoming from the School of Journalism at the People's University of China, published online, said of Murdoch's presentation:

The speech was compiled through painstaking efforts and filled with flattering words from which one could deeply sense the speaker's desire and anxiety to enter the Chinese media market. Aside from Murdoch's attempt to seek material gains, however, many arguments in the speech are poignant and accurate, and they are especially inspiring for us to understand the true value of the media industry.

Murdoch's speech may well have been poignant but something must have been lost in translation so far as his relationship with the Chinese leadership went. For while Murdoch's appearance at the Party School marked perhaps the high point of his relations with Jiang Zemin's previously influential Shanghai clique, it would also mark a turning point in News Corp's fortunes in China.

The fact was that Jiang had gone, replaced in an orderly transition of power by new President and General Secretary of the CCP Hu Jintao. Jiang's departure had also set in train a generational change across the Party and in key government positions. Gone was an entire echelon of officials who had slowly warmed to Murdoch's gracious charms over the years and who had started to open the way for the media tycoon's entry into China.

Murdoch's trip to Beijing on this occasion was again sponsored by the Propaganda Department and the SCIO. But this time the *lao pengyou* who had hosted him in the past were absent. Ding Guangen had also followed his boss into retirement. Zeng Jianhui, head of the SCIO, had been pensioned off to the National People's

Congress (NPC), and Li Bing, our 'go-to man' in previous years, had been moved to a new department.

Despite the high-profile speech to the Party School, a meeting between Murdoch and new President Hu Jintao was conspicuously absent from the trip's agenda. Instead there was a brief and very formal session with Li Changchun, a member of the CCP's inner sanctum, the Politburo's Standing Committee. Hu had elevated the importance of control over the nation's media and information sector by appointing Li as a sort of 'super Propaganda Chief', ranking above even the position Ding Guangen had occupied as head of the Propaganda Department. And unlike Ding, he expressed no love of old Hollywood movies. Instead he repeated the now familiar rhetoric quoted by Beijing officials in meetings with Murdoch. He offered his appreciation to Murdoch 'for his active efforts and strenuous work in advancing cooperation with China's news media' and expressed 'hope that Murdoch and his company, News Corporation, would continue to contribute still more in increasing the mutual understanding between China and the world'.

Murdoch had by now been courting Beijing for over a decade. A year previously he had enjoyed an intimate private dinner with Jiang Zemin. He had by then established a solid working relationship with Ding Guangen, who had indicated during the launch celebrations for the Xing Kong channel that it was just the 'first step' in expanding ties between the two sides. Now the Chinese were back to mouthing platitudes about mutual understanding and cooperation. In China, where *guanxi* and relationships are so important to business, Murdoch had been subject to a comprehensive changing of the guard and appeared to have few contacts inside the new Hu Jintao regime, which was far less inclined to cosy up to the media mogul.

Murdoch was not helping things on his side with yet another re-organisation of the STAR management. In November 2003 a decision was taken to move James Murdoch from Hong Kong to London to take over as CEO of BSkyB. After nearly three years in the job, James had established key relationships with many of the movers and shakers in the China media sector and, from Beijing's point of view, it was clear he enjoyed his father's confidence. In James's place, Murdoch appointed Michelle Guthrie as the new STAR Group CEO. Guthrie, a lawyer by training but a ten-year veteran of the pay television business, had previously been Vice President of Business Development at STAR but had been in Hong Kong just three years before being promoted to the top job. Gone too was Bruce Churchill, STAR's President and Chief Operations Officer who had been with the broadcaster since 1996 and provided valuable support for James during his time. Also departing was Laurie Smith, the sinologist who had worked with me back in 1995 and one of the last News Corp executives with a detailed knowledge of the key players on the Chinese side. Guthrie had the unenviable task of having to step into the shoes of the younger Murdoch while the new Mrs Murdoch, Wendi, peered over her shoulder, as she attempted to advance News Corp's interests in China.

In the other territories where News Corp operated – Australia, the US and the UK – Murdoch had always been a very shrewd judge of politics and had very rarely backed a loser. He loved to talk politics with the editors and journalists he employed, and could astound his political reporters with detailed knowledge of the required electoral swings required in the most marginal of seats. By and large the executives who ran his businesses in those countries were ex-journalists with a nose for politics who were forever 'briefing the boss' on the gossip, rumours and innuendo that were part and parcel of political life. By the end of 2003, Murdoch had no one on the ground in China who either had his ear or could provide an objective evaluation of the complex machinations that were occurring behind the cloistered walls of Zhongnanhai. Too many of his advisers had aligned themselves too closely with Jiang Zemin's Shanghai faction. Murdoch still harboured a rather quaint colonial view of China as a kingdom ruled by an emperor. It may have resembled one under Mao Zedong, and more recently Deng Xiaoping, given the absolute authority they exerted while in power. But Jiang Zemin was just a politician – a highly manipulative one, but a politician nonetheless. He had long been feted by Murdoch, who believed that the President and Communist Party Chief would open China's door to him. Now even though Jiang had stepped aside from all of his official positions – with the exception of the powerful role as Chairman of the Central Military Commission – Murdoch was bestowing on him the same powers of ongoing influence that Jiang's predecessor Comrade Deng had been able to exercise, even from behind the throne for years after he had relinquished all of his official and party positions.

The transfer of power from Jiang to Hu, which had begun in November 2002 at the 16th Party Congress, had been orderly but not without behind-the-scenes rancour. While in power Jiang Zemin had manoeuvred ruthlessly to install members of his faction into positions of power and influence. He had also been criticised by many of his Politburo rivals for his cavalier attitude toward the graft and corruption that compromised many of his Shanghai cohorts, as well as the favouritism shown to his cronies. Hu, by contrast, was largely unaligned to any one faction and was intent on imposing an anti-graft campaign that would combat a growing public dissatisfaction with senior Party officials over what the Chinese media were calling 'the exchange of power for money'.

Hu Jintao also issued new regulations which seemed to be directly aimed at curtailing the activities of the sons and daughters of the now retired Politburo leadership. The new rules demanded that cadres at all levels exercise extreme caution over potential conflicts of interest and also maintain a close watch on the business operations of spouses and children. Hu would not move against Jiang himself, or other Party elders like Ding Guangen, but he was firing a shot across the bows of the princelings to curb their behaviour, while warning the more venal members of Jiang's Shanghai faction that the Party would 'resolutely investigate and punish every single corrupt official that we have discovered'. Among those likely to be caught up in Hu's crackdown on influence pedalling were Jiang Mianheng, son of the former President, and Ding Yucheng, son of Ding Guangen. Both men would barter the influence of their fathers in striking lucrative deals with an eager Rupert Murdoch.

Outside of politics, STAR was also increasingly becoming a victim of its own success. Michelle Guthrie and her China point man, Jamie Davis, were under pressure to emulate the success the broadcaster was achieving in India with its mixture of reality programming, entertainment and game shows. By the end of 2003 STAR was the leading cable broadcaster in India, with close to fifty out of the fifty most-watched programs, and was rapidly expanding its offering with new channels and new genre programming. Subscription and advertising revenues from the South Asia market were doubling year after year. In China, STAR's aggressive move into local production of mass-appeal programming was also building an audience of younger generation Chinese and there was little doubt that its broadcast signal was being pirated and re-transmitted to audiences well beyond its designated landing zone in southern Guangdong province.

But among those watching the Xing Kong channel and its diet of localised US formula television was Liu Yunshan, Ding Guangen's successor as head of the Propaganda Department (or

Publicity Department, as it was now referred to in official statements). Although the newly arranged Department now also boasted a more senior Politburo Standing Committee position, held by Li Changchun, Liu was still responsible for the day-to-day implementation of the controls of China's media. Liu had for ten years been deputy to Ding – the hard-line conservative who eventually came round to Murdoch. Liu, at fifty-seven, was classed as one of the new up-and-coming fourth generation leaders in China and many in the Chinese media sector believed that his ascension to the head of the Propaganda Department would see some relaxation in the iron-fisted controls imposed by his predecessor. They were mistaken.

Liu had another role as head of the Office of the Spiritual Civilisation Steering Committee of the CPC Central Committee. 'Socialist spiritual civilisation' had been a key policy plank of Jiang Zemin's administration, which sought to inculcate and elevate personal and civic morality. New folk heroes were constantly put forward as examples and inspirations to the people. The policy's rationale was that Beijing's leaders were concerned that the West was not only bent on liberalising their country's political and economic systems but was also corrupting its morals.

Liu retained his position at the forefront of the campaign to promote 'spiritual civilisation', which involved instructing the media to publicise the 'virtues of patriotism and observance of law; courtesy and honesty; solidarity and friendship; diligence, frugality and self-improvement; and devotion and contribution'. The role also involved closely monitoring the programming of international broadcasters to guard against 'the spiritual pollution' of Chinese culture through the promotion of decadent Western values.

Although Jiang Zemin had talked a good deal about the need for 'spiritual civilisation', in reality his term in office was marked by a focus on economic growth at all costs while ignoring the resulting environmental and social damage that was occurring. Hu Jintao seemed intent on placing far more emphasis on the fight against 'spiritual pollution' and control of the media.

With the open-door economic policy that had flourished under Jiang there had also been a flow not just of foreign ideas, but of Western cultural mores that were so inculcated in the populist, mass-appeal programming that Murdoch's Xing Kong channel was promoting across China. Shows like *Woman in Control* and *Love Factory* were a long way from the virtues of 'patriotism, frugality and solidarity' that Liu Yunshan's Spiritual Civilisation Steering Committee was supposed to be promoting. In China, what the people wanted was not necessarily what the Party wanted and there was growing criticism in some quarters about the influence of US culture that was seeping into the country via the lounge room television.

Murdoch was buoyed by his invitation to address the Party School. No other media owner had been afforded the same privilege and in his mind, and those of his advisers, the time seemed right to aggressively expand his interests in China — even if it meant venturing beyond the officially sanctioned cable networks of Guangdong to new markets and new audiences. In reality the timing could not have been worse. Just as Murdoch was moving to flex his programming muscle and expand his distribution reach, Hu Jintao's new regime was moving to rein in the media and re-assert control. Murdoch, in the view of many in the Beijing leadership, was fast becoming part of the problem rather than the solution, regarding the opening up of China's media sector.

China's Great Leader Deng Xiaoping had noted the inevitable downside of opening the country to the West when he commented in the early 1990s: 'When you open the windows, you have to live with the flies that come in.'

The problem for Beijing was that by 2004 the flies had become far more of a nuisance than even Deng had envisioned. Like a form of pestilence, the influence of the foreign media companies was growing unabated. The advent of foreign broadcasters had led to a malignancy in the air. President Hu and his sidekicks from the Propaganda Department intended to start swatting flies. Unfortunately for Rupert Murdoch, he was deemed to be one of them.

19

Land of the Giants

Sunk in a plush leather lounge chair before the warm hearth of a hunting lodge on a cold, damp night in the Scottish Highlands, my guest, the President of the *People's Daily* newspaper, Shao Huaze, looked totally content. Hands clasped across his stomach, he was basking in the fire's glow having just savoured an extravagant dinner of the finest Scottish fare – a selection of Aberdeen-Angus beef, grouse, venison, salmon and haggis. Admittedly he had only toyed with the haggis, pushing it about his plate as he attempted to determine its make-up, but he seemed otherwise in an almost stupor of satisfaction.

And so he should have been. It was November 1996 and President Shao had been the week-long guest of Rupert Murdoch in Britain. Shao, who concurrently held the rank of Lieutenant General in the Chinese People's Liberation Army (PLA), was one of the country's most senior and respected ideologues. He had risen through the ranks since joining the PLA in 1950, although his talents lay not as a warrior but as an interpreter of the communist doctrine. In fact his passion outside working hours was the gentle and refined art of traditional calligraphy, in which he was an acknowledged expert. The army general had been appointed to *People's Daily* in 1989 following the Tiananmen Square massacre. His task was to re-instate ideological discipline at the newspaper, whose editorials had briefly indicated a show of support for the student demonstrators prior to the bloody crackdown by the PLA troops. Shao had never been to London or Britain before, and his trip, nominally at the invitation of the London *Times*, was an all-expenses-paid tour designed to show off the best of News Corporation's satellite technology and gain us an ally who would be well placed to influence the policy makers back in Beijing.

Being a recipient of the Murdoch largesse had been quite an experience for the normally austere, softly spoken calligrapher general. There had been four days in a suite at the Ritz Hotel overlooking Green Park, a discreet audience with Prime Minister John Major, private guided tours of the British Museum and Windsor Castle, a day trip to Oxford College, a visit to the News Corp printing plant at Wapping, and dinners at some of London's finest establishments. Murdoch had hosted a dinner for Shao but remained behind in London. It was my role to chaperone our guest on a two-day visit to Scotland. Now, following a chartered private plane flight to Edinburgh and a tour of its famous castle, a chauffeur-driven limousine had delivered our party to a deer hunting lodge in the highlands bordering England where we were to spend the weekend. Fortuitously perhaps, a persistent Scottish drizzle had led President Shao to forego the offer of a spot of deer hunting in favour of a quiet stroll about the grounds prior to dinner. It would have been some picture, though – the PLA general in a deerstalker hat, hunting game on the Scottish highland courtesy of Rupert Murdoch.

As we sat by the fire I offered my esteemed guest a generous tumbler of Scotland's finest single malt whisky, foolishly describing it as a 'Scottish tea' and completely forgetting the general was an avowed teetotaller. He admired the colour and, thinking it was the local equivalent to Chinese jasmine tea, partook of a healthy gulp. Shao leapt to his feet, coughed, spluttered, staggered about and spat the remnants of the whisky on the floor. It was extremely difficult for me to keep a straight face, express concern and offer my apologies at the same time. Still spluttering, the general stomped off to bed. This was not going to look good in my report to Murdoch. I poured myself another drink.

The next day, as our limousine returned us to the airport to catch a chartered flight back to London, I spent the first part of the journey profusely apologising for my mistake regarding 'Scottish tea'. Shao appeared to be accommodating enough and allowed himself a wry smile in response. Having otherwise run out of conversation topics, I turned to Shao and asked him, given his long experience in the Communist Party, the PLA and the media, what advice he would give Rupert Murdoch to ease his way into the China market.

Shao looked out the car window and pondered for some seconds before responding: 'Giants who seek to walk in China need to learn to tread lightly.'

I thought it was profound. I told Murdoch. He stared back blankly. It didn't seem to resonate with him at all. Pity – had he taken this advice he might have ended up in far better stead with the Chinese authorities a decade later.

In China, treading lightly was normally construed as confining your activities to the so-called 'grey sector' – the sort of 'nowhere land' between what Chinese authorities might deem to be strictly legal according to the law and that which would obviously constitute a breach. Operating in the grey sector entails some risk, but risk that could be mitigated so long as one did not stomp about too noisily or push the boundaries too far.

I had been introduced to the concept of the grey sector by President Shao's colleagues at *People's Daily*. When News Corp and *People's Daily* had come together in 1995 in establishing the PDN Xinren joint venture to operate the ChinaByte website, the activities of the company were never strictly legal under China's tight regulations relating to publishing and advertising. As a foreign joint venture, PDN Xinren was not entitled to collect advertising revenue, which I thought might pose something of a problem to our business plan given that advertising was to be the business's sole revenue stream. 'Never mind,' was the response of my *People's Daily* colleagues, 'there is a grey solution.'

The solution in this case was that *People's Daily* owned what was by and large a shelf company, Beijing Hotkey Internet, which did in fact have a licence to collect advertising revenue, although it had never done so. Beijing Hotkey was allocated an office little bigger than a cupboard inside the PDN Xinren head office. Through a series of contractual arrangements, PDN Xinren, with a staff of fifty, provided technology consulting services to Beijing Hotkey with its staff of one. Beijing Hotkey in turn contracted PDN Xinren staff to collect revenue from advertisers to be paid to its account. PDN Xinren then billed Beijing Hotkey for its consulting services, paid for out of revenues collected from companies advertising on the ChinaByte site. Beijing Hotkey never did a thing – it was little more than a cupboard in an office. But the arrangements were made deliberately confusing and designed to keep the various investigators from the Beijing tax department and commercial bureaus scratching their heads for hours on end, but also to provide a solution which could produce a paper trail showing we were operating within the law.

When operating in the grey sector it also helps if you have what the Chinese term 'an umbrella'. An umbrella is a person or organisation in a position of influence who can provide a degree of protection if the authorities came looking to 'rain on your parade'.

In the case of PDN Xinren, *People's Daily* itself provided a sort of umbrella because of its status as the official mouthpiece of the Chinese Communist Party. Even if the various government inspectors twigged that something was not quite right in regard to the various contractual arrangements relating to ChinaByte, they were reluctant to push the matter too far for fear of incurring the wrath of someone higher up the Party hierarchy.

By 2004 STAR desperately needed to expand the distribution of its Mandarin-language satellite television channels beyond its limitations in Guangzhou if it was ever to realise a return on the huge investments it was making in localised programming. It needed to play in the grey sector of the highly regulated and controlled cable television industry in China and Rupert Murdoch concurred. After all, his rivals Viacom, Disney and Time Warner were dipping their toes into the grey sector via various agreements by which they made blocks of programming available to independent cable operators, as a means of expanding distribution and luring new advertisers. But Murdoch was seeking to provide the operators with more than a block of programming – he wanted to offer a bundle of STAR channels, even though the distribution of television channels outside the purview of SARFT was highly illegal. But then Murdoch believed he was in possession of the biggest, strongest umbrella in the country and that his actions would go largely unchecked and unnoticed by the authorities.

Murdoch's decision to allow STAR to push the legal boundaries was largely driven by the economics of the broadcaster's business model. Even though the cost of producing localised Mandarin-language programming for the China market was relatively low, according to STAR TV's Jamie Davis – around US$5000–$30 000 per half hour depending on the format, or about five per cent of what it would cost in the West – coming up with some 700 hours of new programming was costing in the order of US$20 million year. In the US, Murdoch had been an avid disciple of vertical integration whereby, say, Twentieth Century Fox could produce a blockbuster movie for release in cinemas, before its associated production cost could also be amortised through DVD sales, pay-for-view television, distribution to the various Fox cable television operations around the world and other free-to-air television broadcasters. In China he was making programming for what was virtually a single market and a single platform and for an audience that on official figures was limited to no more than two to three million viewers in Guangdong province.

Under a 2002 rule, foreign channels were forced to sell and transmit signals only through a state-run company, China International Television Corp (CITVC). Foreign media companies could sell limited blocks of some programs, such as cartoons and some music shows, to state-owned channels but otherwise CITVC was the only official gateway to the lounge rooms of China. This allowed the authorities to not only restrict the redistribution of the channels to authorised cable systems only, but allowed them to switch the signal off if there was material that they deemed unsuitable for the Chinese audience. Indeed, during my four years in Asia with CNN, this was not an infrequent occurrence when we broadcast material they saw as critical of China or its leadership.

While the Chinese attempted to impose controls on the distribution of foreign channels, the fact remained that the signal was still being beamed down across the entire country from a satellite transponder and it was still possible for any one of the myriad of independent cable operators to use a satellite receiver dish to downlink the signal and redistribute it to their own customers. Given that the majority of foreign channels were encrypted to prevent such pirating of the broadcast channels, the cable operators required a decoder box to unscramble the signals before redistribution. For some years, a good many of the major foreign operators had been aiding and abetting key cable systems owners to 'pirate' the signal by surreptitiously providing them with the necessary decoder boxes. Such 'signal leakage' provided the Western media companies with distribution beyond that which was officially decreed and hopefully would 'seed' a demand for their foreign programming with a new audience, which would in turn put pressure on the authorities to further open up the cable networks to international competition.

The STAR plan being pursued by the broadcaster's new CEO, Michelle Guthrie, and the President of STAR Group China, Jamie Davis, entailed something more than leakage. STAR was offering access to four of its most popular Mandarin-language channels – Xing Kong, Channel V (Music), National Geographic Channel and a Movie Channel – via a head-end decoder box which would allow the cable operators to decode and redistribute the signals and insert their advertising if necessary. For this, STAR was demanding payment, based on either an annual subscription fee for smaller operators or a share of subscription revenues for larger cable systems with in excess of 2000 customers. Because these decoder boxes were 'addressable', individual set-top units could be turned on or off by STAR if the cable operators failed to pay the fees.

The problem was that even if it were legal to distribute the channels, other laws barred STAR from collecting 'subscription' revenues or lease payments from the cable operators. To get around the issue, the Beijing Hotkey Internet 'cupboard' was brought out of retirement. Although News Corp had by this time sold off its interest in PDN Xinren and the ChinaByte website, it had retained ownership of Beijing Hotkey Internet because of its valuable licence to receive payments for advertising services. Because Beijing Hotkey needed to be 100 per cent Chinese-owned to satisfy legal requirements, several of STAR's Chinese employees based at the new Shanghai office were engaged as 'directors' and 'company officials'.

In late 2003 and early 2004, STAR accelerated its push into the grey sector of satellite channel distribution with an expanding team of sales representatives fanning out across the country targeting regional cable services, residential compounds and hotels, from Xinjiang in the west to Shanghai in the east. Through a complex series of contractual arrangements, invoices were issued in the name of Beijing Hotkey and payments received in the form of cash or cheques from the cable operators for 'advertising services', before the monies were eventually channelled back to STAR.

STAR was certainly pushing the boundaries of what was deemed to be legally acceptable behaviour. But Murdoch, Guthrie and the various China advisers now employed by News Corp all seemed to be operating under the assumption that their 'Beijing umbrella' offered a level of protection that was not afforded to other international broadcasters in the sector. After all, with the forced resignation of Time Warner chief Jerry Levin, following the disastrous merger with AOL, there was no other media company with better Beijing relationships than News Corp. Murdoch's exalted view that he could continue to operate with a degree of immunity was only further bolstered when the son of antagonist-turned-ally Ding Guangen came calling with a proposal that promised to be the media tycoon's biggest break yet in the China market.

Ding Yucheng was, like his father, an avid bridge player of international standing. He would often partner the elder Ding in bridge tournaments against other Politburo members inside the Zhongnanhai compound and occasionally travelled overseas to play in international competitions. As one of the Communist Party 'princelings' he was much in demand to sit on the boards of aspiring media companies for the influence he might be able to bring to bear on matters relating to the Propaganda Department's deliberations.

Even though his father had officially retired from his position as head of the department by the end of 2004, Ding Yucheng was still seeking to bargain any perceived influence he might still have into personal financial gain.

The Ding Yucheng proposal was being sponsored by Murdoch's new government relations adviser, Liu Heung Shing, or HS Liu as he was more widely known. HS was a former Pulitzer-prize winning news photographer who had worked throughout Asia, as well as the former Soviet Union, for both *Time* magazine and the Associated Press. To date, Liu is the only photojournalist of Chinese descent to have won the coveted prize. More recently he had parlayed his China connections to re-invent himself as a government liaison officer, first with Time Warner – where he had played a key role in the coordination of the 1998 Fortune Global Forum in Shanghai – and now, having jumped ship, with News Corp in China.

HS Liu had undoubtedly good connections in the office of former President Jiang Zemin. He was also close to Jiang's son, Mianheng, and the clique of senior Shanghai Communist Party officials who had prospered the former Chinese leader. HS had established a good rapport with Wendi Deng Murdoch and provided introductions to the key players in Shanghai. He was an ardent exponent of the view that even though Jiang Zemin had stepped down from his official positions, his influence still extended into every corner of Chinese politics.

The approach to STAR, and ultimately Rupert Murdoch, was

predicated by a change in the Propaganda Department's policy with regard to foreign investment in program production in China. Worried about the proliferation of new television channels but the relatively poor quality of local programming, the Beijing leadership issued new regulations in October 2004 which would allow foreign investment in Chinese film and television production companies. In reality the new laws were designed to attract what the Chinese coveted most – money, managerial and technical know-how, and attractive content. Titled the *Interim Regulations on the Administration of Sino-Foreign Joint and Cooperative Ventures in Broadcast Television Program Production Operating Enterprises*, the new rules still required that the Chinese partner retain at least 51 per cent control of the enterprise and also forbade joint venture television enterprises from producing news programs.

Ding Yucheng, however, believed it was possible to utilise the new regulations to achieve a sort of back-door takeover of a small satellite television channel based in a remote part of western China but with a signal footprint well beyond its current capacity. Qinghai Satellite TV Station already reached cable systems in northwest China and several major cities around the country, including large parts of the capital Beijing, giving it a potential audience of some 100 million people – well above what STAR was achieving in both official and unofficial distribution terms. Under the deal, which was personally signed off by Murdoch after a meeting with Ding Yucheng, News Corp would pump some US$40 million into a company called Runde Investment, which was controlled by the Communist Party princeling. Runde would in turn acquire a 49 per cent stake in Qinghai Satellite as part of an arrangement whereby it would lease the station's channel capacity. Runde would then fill the channel with STAR programming that had been produced for Xing Kong but which was otherwise officially restricted to the cable systems of Guangdong province. Legally, Qinghai Satellite would still be seen to be controlling the content, although in reality it would be a surrogate STAR channel. Given that Qinghai Satellite would essentially remain a 51 per cent Chinese-controlled entity it was subject to none of the restrictions that had been imposed on foreign broadcasters and hence opened up a whole new audience for Murdoch's aspirations in China. HS Liu was so convinced of the merits of the deal and the apparent protection that he envisaged would come about through the connections to the Jiang family, as well as Ding Yucheng's involvement, that he intended to resign from News Corp to take up a position with the new enterprise.

To complete the transaction, News Corp entered into a second joint venture to sell advertising on behalf of its new Qinghai Satellite TV Station. It structured a deal with a subsidiary of the Chinese Communist Youth League to form an advertising company with the role of representing Qinghai Satellite in the all-important commercial centre of Shanghai. The League, with some 70 million members aged between fourteen and twenty-eight, was a powerful and influential force in Chinese business and political circles.

Murdoch believed that he was on the brink of a spectacular breakthrough in China. In an analysts' briefing in early 2005 he went so far as to go on record and announce that his company had invested in a new Chinese venture, 'where we'll have nearly 50 per cent . . . of a prime-time channel, which will have, you know, access to well over 100 million homes'. He had good reason to be confident. Murdoch was not only the best-connected media mogul in China but now here he was as business partner with the son of the feared Ding Guangen and in bed with one of the most powerful Communist Party organisations in the country. On past reckoning, Murdoch should have been the beneficiary of an 'umbrella' that offered protection of unrivalled proportions.

Not every STAR executive was as enthusiastic about the deal as Rupert and Wendi, however. Jamie Davis expressed reservations about the risks involved and the danger of upsetting the national regulators by doing a deal at a local level that bypassed state controls. However, the deal had the backing of Michelle Guthrie as well as HS Liu, who continued to cite his extensive connections to Jiang Zemin and the younger Ding's involvement as virtual guarantees of success. Murdoch consulted his coterie of China advisers about the proposal, including the new London *Times* editor Robert Thompson, himself a former Beijing correspondent and, like his boss, now married to a Chinese national. Everyone was in agreement that it was an opportunity too good to be passed up.

However, in their impatience to take advantage of the newly

constituted broadcasting outlet, the STAR executives began broadcasting its Mandarin-language programming on the Qinghai Satellite Channel in January 2005. Unfortunately, they had not sought the necessary prior approval from SARFT, which required that all foreign-produced programming be vetted prior to broadcast. The Qinghai Satellite TV management were roundly rapped over the knuckles for breaching regulations but the STAR executives regarded this as only a minor violation that their undoubtedly good contacts could easily smooth over with the authorities. However, the incident was referred by SARFT to its overseers at the Propaganda Department and in particular to Liu Yunshan, who as head of the Spiritual Civilisation Steering Committee was becoming increasingly concerned about the content of foreign-produced programming that was being cloned and copied by local television stations across the country. A programming schedule that comprised game shows and reality television not only fell short of espousing Communist Party values but failed to touch upon the widely-regarded Confucian values of collective morality: love, suffering, filial piety and redemption. Liu Yunshan began to express publicly his concerns for 'national cultural security'.

Within a month of the Qinghai Satellite TV broadcast, SARFT, at the Propaganda Department's direction, issued a new notice dated 25 February 2005, which marked a significant step back from the previous open-hearted embrace of foreign involvement in China's film and television production that had been announced just a few months before. Entitled *Circular Regarding Matters Relating to the Implementation of the Temporary Provisions on the Administration of Sino-Foreign Investment and Cooperative Joint Venture Television Program Production Enterprises*, the notice had two aims: to prevent foreign corporations from entering any more than one joint venture with a Chinese production partner, and to re-impose strict controls over the content of proposed programming. It read:

> While we encourage the working concept and method of maturing the market for foreign program production, we must control the contents of all products of joint ventures in a practical manner, understand the political inclinations and background of foreign joint venture parties, and in this way prevent harmful foreign ideology and culture from entering the realm of our television program production through joint investment and cooperation.

The following month, on 13 March, Murdoch was back in China at the official invitation of the SCIO, but this time the old faces who had become friends were long gone. He met with Liu Yunshan at the Propaganda Department in what those present described as a polite but formal meeting. The official statement issued after the meeting was notable for the words chosen to reflect the tone of the exchange between the two men. The Chinese side stated that Liu had 'encouraged media mogul Rupert Murdoch and his company News Corporation to make more substantial efforts to enhance mutual understanding between China and the rest of the world'. Given the degree to which Murdoch had gone to placate the Chinese over the past thirteen years it appeared that, according to the new regime, the News Corp chairman still had a way to go to prove his *bona fides*.

Murdoch's formal response was that News Corp would 'further strengthen cooperative ties with the Chinese media, and explore new areas with an *even more positive attitude*'.

Murdoch had his detractors inside the Chinese Politburo who continued to argue that he had little interest in China or her people other than as a means of making money. His Chinese commercial rivals, who feared his reputation as a consummate deal-maker intent on taking control of the lucrative Chinese television market for himself, played on those sentiments. 'China is for the Chinese', they would argue, and everything that could be done should be done to prevent the foreign devil Murdoch from making his fortune in a market that was rightfully theirs. Liu Yunshan was sending a message to Murdoch that he needed to do more to prove his credentials.

But Murdoch was not listening, just as he failed to take heed of the advice proffered by *People's Daily*'s astute President nearly a decade earlier. This was no friendly giant treading delicately through the regulatory fields of the Chinese media landscape. This was the Incredible Hulk on steroids – pumped up by his own self-belief and urged on by his advisers, he was stepping on toes everywhere. Murdoch's indelible trail could be seen well beyond the grey area as he strayed into a sector the Chinese authorities definitely considered 'black'. Murdoch the media giant was heading for a tumble.

20

Hitting the Wall

We were lucky to be alive. Our black Audi sedan lay half buried beneath a hillock of Beijing topsoil, rich with what might best be described as organic matter. The car's windscreen had popped, the side windows were smashed and, sitting in the front passenger seat, I had a moment of panic when I realised I could not move my arms or legs. It was only when I opened my eyes that I saw that the car had filled almost to chest level with the black, pungent soil, pinning us to our seats. A few metres away the smoking hulk of the truck that had been carrying the load lay upturned on its side, the driver scrambling groggily through an open window. With some assistance from local passers-by, I extracted myself from the vehicle, shook the dirt from my clothing and surveyed the crash site.

Several hours earlier, adviser Laurie Smith and I had been deep in torturous negotiation with our *People's Daily* counterparts in relation to the proposed joint venture with News Corp, struggling to overcome an impasse on funding arrangements. It being a Saturday, and coming after a week-long round of discussions, our Chinese hosts suggested a picnic outing might provide a welcome break and the opportunity to talk over issues in a more relaxed atmosphere. Two black, locally assembled chauffeur-driven Audi sedans had been commandeered from the *People's Daily* car pool and the planned rendezvous was a popular waterfall site some 80 kilometres north of the capital.

But our outing did not quite go to plan. Beijing's Saturday lunchtime peak hour, coupled with a sudden rain shower, ensured that our journey got off to a slow start. It took some two hours to wend our way through the traffic that had gridlocked the ring roads that lead from the capital's centre before linking to the main highway some 10 kilometres distant. However, having negotiated the worst of the traffic we were finally on the highway making our way north, our driver accelerating – too quickly to my mind – past lines of trucks, carts and assorted farmers' wagons, as we hit what we thought was the open road to our destination.

Sitting in the front passenger seat of the lead car of our little convoy, I noticed that ahead of us, travelling in the opposite direction down an otherwise straight section of road, came a Chinese dump truck loaded with soil and towing an equally encumbered trailer in its wake. From a side road, a small car made as if to cross the highway, sticking its nose out onto the highway. The truck driver braked and swerved. Unfortunately, in the wet conditions following

the rain, his truck and trailer jack-knifed and now the entire juggernaut was skidding sideways out of control – covering the full
width of the highway and heading directly towards our vehicle.
I watched proceedings as if in slow motion as the distance between
the Audi and the truck rapidly closed. I shut my eyes for what I
could only believe would be a near fatal outcome.

But instead of the scream of metal on metal there was just an
almighty thump, followed by blackness. At almost the very last
moment the truck and trailer tipped onto its side, spewing its entire
load of Beijing's finest organic topsoil onto the road in front of
it, where it acted as a sort of giant cushion absorbing the impact
as our car slammed into it. All of us in the vehicle walked away
unscathed – apart from having a degree of soil lodged in various
bodily orifices for some days to come. Our trip had come to a
grinding halt. We decided to return to town, regroup and consider
our options.

In retrospect, that near disastrous outing is an apt metaphor for
Rupert Murdoch's adventures in China. He too had taken considerable time to navigate his way around the bureaucratic blocks put
in his way by the Beijing leadership before News Corp believed it
had found the way clear to accelerate past its rivals, on the way to
taking a lucrative slice of the nation's satellite and cable television
market. But in mid-2005, Murdoch's STAR ambitions would also
crash into an unyielding obstacle.

The new Chinese regime believed Murdoch's ambitions were

gaining pace at too fast a rate, and acted decisively to counter them. First, in June of 2005, the Beijing Industrial and Commercial Bureau raided the office of the STAR subsidiary, Beijing Hotkey Internet, seizing files and decoder boxes as well as impounding the passport of the broadcaster's Vice President for Channel Distribution, Tan Yadong. Tan was a feisty, ambitious 43-year-old mainland Chinese with good connections who had previously worked for Time Warner in Beijing, where he had exhibited no lack of confidence in his own abilities. Enticed away to STAR, Tan was a driving force behind the push into China's grey sector. But now the Chinese regulators announced that they were investigating the STAR operation for selling illegal access to satellite television.

Tan had not helped himself, or News Corp's cause, when in a July 2003 interview with the Asian *Wall Street Journal* he had boasted about STAR's ability 'to bend the rules' and told how his managers actively coached reticent cable television owners about ways of exploiting a regulatory loophole that allowed the operator to get around the state ban on carrying foreign broadcasters. The article also implied that the main regulator, SARFT, had largely been ineffective in policing government policy aimed at preventing consumers from watching unauthorised foreign programming, and seemed unwilling or unable to take action against the leakage of STAR programming to the regional cable operators. It was akin to speeding past a traffic policeman and thumbing your nose at his inability to catch you. In hindsight, it was surely a serious error of judgment to be critical of SARFT in the conduct of its duties. It is a mistake to humiliate a Chinese government department in public – it is tantamount to a loss of 'face' and the Chinese regulators have long memories. The maintenance of face, or *mianzi*, is a crucial aspect of China's social relationships, reflecting a measure of power, influence and status in terms of society's positive assessment of a person.

At the time, Tan was probably justifiably confident of STAR's ability to continue the roll-out of its unauthorised programming, given it was still too soon for the incoming Hu Jintao regime to move against Jiang Zemin's 'old friend' Rupert Murdoch. But the newspaper article and relentless bragging by some senior STAR executives set in train a series of complaints by Murdoch's rivals – both international and domestic – about the seemingly 'special treatment' being meted out to him.

By the northern winter of 2004, Hu Jintao felt emboldened enough to start moving against many of Jiang's 'Shanghai Gang'. One of those was Xu Guangchun, the Director of SARFT. Xu was an amiable career journalist and avid amateur photographer who had formed a close relationship with the former President Jiang Zemin while heading the Xinhua news agency in Shanghai, prior to 1988. His move to the Beijing office of Xinhua coincided with Jiang's assumption of the top post following the Tiananmen Square incident. He was also an associate of Ding Guangen and after being appointed as SARFT Director in 2000, Xu pursued a policy of the gradual opening of China's media sector to foreign investment – a program which favoured Murdoch and brought the two men together on a number of occasions. Xu had been an active supporter of News Corp's entry into the China market and in 2001 had signed off on the decision to permit STAR to broadcast its Xing Kong channel into the cable systems of Guangdong province. It was Xu who also pushed through the new regulations of October of 2004 which allowed for foreign media companies to own up to 49 per cent of a Sino-foreign joint venture television production company, opening the way for the US$40 million Murdoch deal with Ding Yucheng and the Qinghai Satellite Television channel. And it was Xu who was ousted just a couple of months later by Hu Jintao – sent back to the provinces as a Party Chief and replaced by Wang Taihua, a long-time provincial Communist Party cadre with no media experience at all.

Wang immediately set about rolling back the reforms that had been initiated by Xu. In February 2005, SARFT issued the new notice restricting foreign media companies to just one joint production deal and re-imposing strict controls on programming content. SARFT also deliberately slowed down the processing of applications already in the pipeline from the big media players seeking approval for joint venture production proposals – including those from Disney, Viacom, Sony, Warner Brothers, and Australia's Seven Network.

For those of us in the industry following events in Beijing,

Wang's February edict appeared to be a deliberate salvo for the attention of Murdoch. It was a signal that SARFT wanted Murdoch to ease off the accelerator.

But Qinghai Satellite Television began broadcasting STAR programming before it had been approved, and prior to any authorisation of any cooperation between News Corp and the station itself. Murdoch's unauthorised push was largely a result of his impatience to prove the naysayers wrong and to prove that the mainland market would be the financial bonanza he had always predicted. But he and his executives had misread the change in the Chinese leadership's attitude. Murdoch's action played into the hands of his commercial competitors who could legitimately point at him and claim that he 'could not be trusted'. Moreover, they justifiably began to pepper SARFT with queries about why their rival was being allowed to flout the law.

Wang had no immediate answer to such accusations – nor should he have had. He had no previous relationship with Murdoch. In fact he had had no previous relationship with the media at all, having spent nearly his entire career as a senior Communist Party apparatchik in some of the country's more outlying provinces. But he now had a directive from Hu Jintao's new leadership team that SARFT needed to reel in the reforms put in place by his predecessor and re-impose strict controls on the Chinese media sector.

On a trip to Beijing in the northern Spring of 2005, my own contacts at the Propaganda Department and SARFT, who in the past had been well disposed towards Murdoch and News Corp, expressed considerable dismay over the media mogul's current activities in China. From their point of view, the Chinese authorities had made very significant concessions to Murdoch in return for what was always politely termed his 'strenuous efforts to promote China to the outside world'. They argued that no other foreign media company was better positioned or enjoyed more access than News Corp. Of the thirty-one foreign channels that were permitted by the Chinese authorities to be distributed to three-star hotels and above, official compounds and international residential areas, nine were either directly or partly owned by Murdoch. Additionally two of the channels, Xing Kong and Phoenix, had been granted landing rights in Guangdong province. News Corp had been the first foreign media company to be granted approval to establish a representative office in Beijing and the first to be given approval to open a second office in the country's commercial hub of Shanghai. That Murdoch's STAR was now actively engaged in a campaign to circumvent the intent of the SARFT regulations relating to the distribution of satellite television channels, and encouraging cable operators to bend the rules, was beyond the comprehension of the Chinese regulatory authorities.

The Propaganda Department and SARFT were being given the impression that Murdoch was showing contempt for the regulators and was a 'law unto himself'. He was backing them into a corner where they were losing face in terms of relations with both the foreign and domestic media. SARFT was also losing *mianzi* with Hu Jintao and the leadership clique, who were questioning why the national regulator appeared powerless to exert control over the provincial media operators.

Mianzi is a social phenomenon practised from the grassroots level all the way up to international relationships between nations and governments. Inherent in the concept is an obligation to avoid putting an individual, an organisation, or even a government, in a position or situation whereby they might lose face. It is normally demonstrated in Chinese culture by a tendency to avoid conflict by refraining from public criticism of one another, or bringing up embarrassing facts in the public domain.

Now, Murdoch was playing the province against the state. Ultimately, his actions were causing Hu and his new leadership team to lose *mianzi*.

The opportunity to install a roadblock in front of Murdoch's speeding ambitions came when a disgruntled former STAR channel distribution manager, Jiang Hua, went public with revelations about Murdoch's machinations in the grey sector of satellite channel distribution. Jiang Hua had resigned as an employee of STAR in March 2004 after an alleged disagreement with Jamie Davis, but agreed to continue to market the broadcaster's channels. In early 2005 he became involved in a bitter dispute over monies he claimed were owed to him by Tan Yadong. When Tan gave no indication of being prepared to settle, Jiang took his story to the local media.

In it he gave details of how STAR circumvented SARFT regulations and cajoled cable system operators into exploiting various loopholes, and detailed the way in which subscription payments were disguised by channelling them through the Beijing Hotkey shelf company.

The regulators were being chastised by their own media for having failed to detect and act on STAR's manoeuvrings. In June the uniformed officers of the Beijing Industrial and Commercial Bureau's Dongcheng district branch, which had jurisdiction over News Corp's Beijing office, conducted the raid in which they took away documents and decoder boxes relating to Beijing Hotkey as part of an investigation 'to determine whether it leased satellite channels illegally'. The international media took up the story and an increasingly vehement Jiang Hua continued to sprout details of News Corp's activities to all who would listen, telling *Time* magazine: 'News Corp called what I did grey-market distribution. But it wasn't grey. It was black.'

But it was an article in *People's Daily* of 13 July 2005 under the headline 'China Bans Foreign Participation in Domestic TV Channels' which provided stark proof that the Murdoch juggernaut had collided with a roadblock. The report, also covered by other official media organisations including the Xinhua News Agency, stated that SARFT had issued new regulations which 'banned any cooperation in channel operation between local TV and radio stations and foreign companies'.

There was no attempt at face-saving compromise or refraining from public criticism. The new regulations stipulated that all local TV and radio stations should not rent their channels to foreign companies and also should not cooperate with foreign companies in running channels. It went on to order that all other kinds of cooperation with foreign companies should first be approved by SARFT's provincial branches.

In order to remove any doubt as to which 'foreign company' they were referring to in particular, the authorities ensured the final paragraph of the news items read: 'SARFT advises that the Qinghai Satellite TV Station in western China had ceased its cooperation with the News Corporation held by Rupert Murdock [sic] which started early this year.'

Murdoch's 'car wreck' had gone public. For Murdoch and the princeling son of Party elder Ding Guangen to have been so openly rapped over the knuckles meant the decision to do so had been cleared at the highest levels of the Beijing leadership. It signalled that whatever protective umbrella had been in place prior to Jiang Zemin's retirement and the arrival of Hu Jintao had all but dissolved. Murdoch's insatiable appetite for the Chinese market, and the unbridled enthusiasm of STAR CEO Michelle Guthrie and her STAR China President, Jamie Davis, to please their boss, had led them to push too hard, too fast, too soon – and they had crashed.

Three weeks later, when the new regulations were officially promulgated by SARFT, the regulators also moved to put a halt to operations like those of Tan Yadong, which were directly soliciting cable network operators to surreptitiously take the STAR channels. SARFT was now demanding that all contact between Chinese radio and television stations and foreigners be subject to the 'administration, guidance, and supervision' of provincial-level People's Government Foreign Affairs Offices and the SARFT Foreign Affairs Department.

Murdoch had indeed stirred up a hornet's nest of reaction. But the Chinese authorities were not finished. On 2 August 2005 the Propaganda Department issued additional regulations covering every aspect of the media in China under the auspices of 'safeguarding the national cultural security', which were in reality an attempt to stem the tide of foreign influence seeping into the country. There would be no more opening up of the Chinese television market. Instead the Propaganda Department decreed that henceforth the authorities would not issue any new approvals for foreign satellite television channels to be broadcast in China and would increase supervision of channels that had already received authorisation. It reiterated the ban on individuals purchasing television satellite dishes without government permission and announced that the regulators would 'increase control over content censorship' of imported television series, programs and animated features.

The following week News Corp went into damage control amid a great deal of finger-pointing and 'I told you so' discussions between the Hong Kong-based executives and the Murdochs in New York.

There was a flurry of management change that News Corp hoped might placate the Chinese authorities. Michelle Guthrie announced that Jamie Davis would be departing to take up a new position in Singapore with an ESPN–STAR Sports joint venture. Davis was widely thought to have welcomed the move – he had been somewhat disgruntled at having been passed over for the top job at STAR in favour of Guthrie and had often resented her interference in the running of the China operations. Under the new arrangements Guthrie herself would assume Davis's responsibilities, although she also announced the appointment of Wei Zhang to the newly created position of Chief Operating Officer of STAR China. Wei was a confidant of Wendi Deng Murdoch and, like her, she had an MBA from a top US university and an impressive pedigree as consultant to Bain & Company, finance specialist with GE Capital, and TV personality for CCTV in China. It would be her role to try to mend fences in Beijing – and report back to Wendi.

Tan Yadong was largely left to fend for himself. Although Tan's department had been one of the most successful STAR divisions in China, bringing in revenue amounting to several millions of dollars, the executives in Hong Kong offered not a word in his defence nor acknowledged that he was simply doing his job. Instead the STAR spokesman would only state that the company's legal advice was that it should say nothing about the investigation. Tan was identified in the international media as the apparent villain in STAR's push into the darker corners of China's grey sector. He left the company soon after, gravely disappointed at what he saw as the lack of loyalty shown to him by an employer which had previously praised him for his outstanding achievements.

Ding Yucheng closed the office of Runde Investments soon after. News Corp never disclosed how much of the US$40 million investment in Qinghai Satellite Television channel it was able to recover, nor the amount paid to Ding Yucheng as a consultant to the project.

Neither Murdoch nor Michelle Guthrie had raised the Qinghai deal with their Phoenix joint venture partner, Liu Changle, who had undoubtedly the best high-level Beijing contacts of any media player. In an interview with *The Sydney Morning Herald* soon after the banning of new foreign broadcasters, Liu said Guthrie had only mentioned it to him after it was under way.

'At that point I thought it would be difficult based on the current policy,' Liu says. 'But I was thinking that maybe a breakthrough or a miracle could happen, because it was Rupert.'

Liu said there was some ambiguity in the rules and Murdoch would have been calculating that pure entertainment programming like Xing Kong would not have raised any party hackles. But tolerance, Liu said, 'hadn't reached the degree that Rupert had expected'.

Indeed, all tolerance had evaporated.

At a media conference in New York on 16 September, a chastened Murdoch conceded that News Corp had 'hit a brick wall in China'.

'A year ago I would have said there's a lot of opening up going on,' Murdoch said. 'The present trend is the reverse. The authorities are now quite paranoid about what gets through.'

Murdoch went on to argue that he believed there was a limit to how much the Chinese government could control the influx of foreign content, citing the availability of pirated Hollywood movies in China.

'They can see in these films how Americans live, how people live in other parts of the world. They are a very intelligent people. That's got to have a lasting effect which the government can't control.'

Murdoch was returning to the same themes he had raised in the fateful Whitehall speech twelve years earlier. Once again he was suggesting, perhaps with more subtlety, that 'satellite technology was an unambiguous threat to totalitarian regimes'. Murdoch's frustration with the Chinese authorities was showing through. Despite his best efforts, Beijing was still refusing to yield the very control Murdoch had so famously believed would be undermined by modern communication technology. In many ways, he was back where he started from.

There was no doubt the media tycoon had been right about the potential value of the Chinese television market he had perceived a decade or more earlier. Just a month after his admission that his company had hit a brick wall in China, the Hunan Satellite Television Channel broadcast the final episode of an unashamed imitation of the *American Idol* talent show that STAR's Xing Kong channel had brought to China. Sponsored by a dairy company, the *Mongolian Cow Sour Yogurt Super Girl Concert* attracted some 400 million viewers – making it the largest television audience in Chinese history and, inevitably, the largest domestic TV audience in the world. The eventual winner, the 21-year-old tomboy Li Yuchun, received 32.5 million SMS viewer votes. The Chinese media were reporting that advertising slots for the final were being sold at the rate of US$15 000 a second.

'China is vast, but China has not opened up yet. We keep a presence there. We're going to behave ourselves and be there until we see a change in policies. And it will have to come. It's a sovereign country, and that's the way they do things, and we'll just wait,' Murdoch told a media conference in Los Angeles in February 2007.

Here was Rupert Murdoch finally conceding that the Chinese pot of gold he had pursued so relentlessly remained tantalisingly out of reach.

21

The Wendi Factor

The Core Club, on East 55th Street in downtown New York, is regarded as one of the city's swankiest and most exclusive private enclaves. Its invitation-only membership – chosen elite from fields such as art, architecture, media, politics, finance, technology and sport – get to pay upwards of US$75 000 to join and US$12 000 a year in order to rub shoulders with their fellow leaders of American society, amid a contrived setting of timbered walls and leather couches fit for the super-rich.

Checking in is completed by offering a fingerprint to a biometric scanner. There is a library where one can browse soon-to-be-published books, a screening room to view soon-to-be-released movies, and an art gallery. The club's timbered walls are adorned with contemporary artworks by the likes of de Kooning and Basquiat, lent by club members from their private collections to provide an appropriate ambience to the setting. A dedicated 'Core Consultant' is on hand to provide the services of a 'personal experience manager', ensuring, according to the club's brochure, that each member 'paints their own unique and vibrant picture of modern life'.

The Core Club's vision is less than modest. It seeks to establish an 'international community that would transform contemporary culture as radically as Starbucks has transformed the way we think about coffee and as profoundly as the iPod has changed the way we consume media'.

It was here on the evening of Thursday, 27 April 2006 that Rupert and Wendi Murdoch co-hosted a lavish book party to honour the author and self-styled 'personal growth and spiritual counsellor', Kathy Freston. That the book in question should be titled *The One: Finding Soul Mate Love and Making It Last* would have surprised Murdoch detractors who have long seen him as the ultimate hard-nosed, ruthless dealmaker little given to sentiment or spirituality. That Wendi was singing the praises of the book which draws upon Buddhism and Hinduism, espouses a routine of prayers, mantras and meditation, and which calls upon readers to 'move towards wholeness by regarding your partner as an extension of God', perhaps provided insight into the unlikely relationship between the media mogul and his Chinese princess.

The Murdoch invitees at the book party represented the A-list of New York high society and included the designer Calvin Klein, actress Patti D'Arbanville, screenwriter Mitch Glazer and his wife, actress Kelly Lynch, film director Brian Grazer, publisher of *Vanity*

Fair Graydon Carter, Hollywood studio head Harvey Weinstein, supermodel Frederique, record producer Ahmet Ertegun, *Rolling Stone* magazine's Jann Wenner, CBS Television chief Les Moonves, singer-songwriter Carole Bayer Sager and her husband Bob Daly, the former chairman of Warner Brothers. The Murdochs had gone to considerable trouble and expense to celebrate what many would have dismissed as just another 'new age' book on relationships.

Freston had, in truth, become one of Wendi's closest friends and confidants. They had a lot in common. At the time of the book launch both were in their late thirties, tall, svelte and attractive, and both had come through a series of failed prior relationships before finding their 'One'. In Kathy Freston's case, she found her soul mate in husband Tom Freston, one of the founders of the MTV Music Television and, until his sacking by Sumner Redstone in late 2006, the Chief Executive of Viacom, still one of the US's largest media conglomerates. Both women had married media tycoons who were considerably older than themselves – twenty years in the case of the Frestons, while thirty-seven years separate Rupert and Wendi Murdoch. But Wendi was co-hosting the party as much out of friendship as her belief in the principles espoused in the book.

Chapter one of the Freston book begins:

The One. The love of our life, the fulfilment of our dreams. That glorious person who will set our soul on fire and stoke our passion for life. We get up in the morning to the song of this promise on the radio and lull ourselves to sleep at night with novels and films about two disenchanted people who finally find each other and, in the process, make the world a better place. We hope against hope that one day this will be our story. We long for this connection we've heard about, with all its magic and mystery and mojo; we want to be lit up and transformed simply by being in the presence of that heaven-sent one and only. Ah, soul mate love.

Asked by a journalist from *The New Yorker* at the party what she thought of the book, Wendi replied, 'I am not a very spiritual person, but I would like to be. I read the book and kept thinking, That's me! That's me!'

Murdoch, who was beside her at the time of the interview, conceded that as a result of his wife's reading of the book she had persuaded him to take up yoga, which he was now practising two or three times a week.

'She's my great help and adviser,' he added affectionately.

In terms of China, Wendi Deng Murdoch has certainly played the role of adviser to her husband in his myriad machinations designed to turn mainland television broadcasting into another part of his ever expanding media empire. The degree to which she has been a 'great help' is arguable.

When Rupert married Wendi the talk was that the media magnate's new bride would open doors for News Corporation's ambitious expansion plans in China. She spoke the language, understood the culture and had the ear of most powerful media executive in the world. But while she brought to the partnership an insight into the cultural and often complex nuances of doing business there, she had no head for the politics of the country's opaque and evolving political environment.

Wendi Deng had left China for the US as a naïve 20-year-old from the provinces. By the time she returned to work full-time for STAR TV in 1997 she had completed an MBA at Yale, but had never worked for a media company nor for any other company on the mainland. She had no business connections in China, no powerful *guanxi* at the political level that were going to open doors for her. She was given the task of trying to improve the distribution of STAR TV's Channel V music channel in China. Wendi would come to my office in Beijing at the time and ask for advice. I would attempt to explain the complexities of the country's political and regulatory hierarchy and unwieldy regulatory framework within which News Corp had to operate. She would appear frustrated that somehow her 'Chinese-ness' was not enough in itself to broker deals with the nation's cable television operators. She understood the business but struggled to grasp the politics. But Wendi did have gall and there were few people she would not front if she thought they could assist her progress. None of us who worked alongside her ever had the opportunity to see just how good she was at being Vice President – Business Development, the role stated on her business card, because within a year of starting work she was well on the way to becoming the next Mrs Murdoch. She had stepped into a new league.

Once Wendi Deng's relationship with Murdoch had been established, there was little doubt she had the boss's ear. In January 2000 she was complicit in the departure of Murdoch's rainmaker Chief Executive, Gareth Chang, after having served just eighteen months in the job. She had correctly deduced that he had over-promised and under-delivered in terms of increasing STAR TV's access to the mainland market. Chang had also made the mistake of trying to sideline the boss's wife from the China operations. It was Wendi who finally convinced her husband that Chang had to go. She also teamed up with new stepson James Murdoch to initiate and advocate the Chinese internet investments amounting to some US$45 million — nearly all of which were later written off as total losses.

When Wendi first returned to China after her marriage to Murdoch in June 1999, she did so in company with her husband and as such was largely treated by the Chinese as an appendage to the powerful media tycoon — and little else. But in 2001, when she returned in her own right to assist James in the acquisition of a spate of internet companies and start-ups, Wendi began to find her own feet and establish a trusted circle of friends that went well beyond that of her spouse's business and political connections. She started to socialise with a coterie of young, US-educated Chinese graduates – bilingual and bicultural – who had been lured back to China by the promise of fortunes to be made in the nation's rapidly expanding economy. In the late 1990s and early 2000s, their corporate acumen and knowledge of Western business practices were in high demand by the up-and-coming Chinese telecommunications, banking and investment corporations which were riding a wave of expansive growth and looking to privatise by way of floating on international stock markets.

These US university alumni were easily distinguishable from their mainland counterparts. Like Wendi, they were stylish and sophisticated, dressed in designer fashions with brand name accessories, preferred cappuccino to green tea and red wine to maotai, often favoured a plate of pasta over a bowl of rice, and hung out in the most chic nightclubs. There was a degree of elitism amongst them which often offended the mainlanders who worked alongside them but had not yet found their own way to the outside world. But among the other values these young overseas Chinese shared was a sort of patriotism, in that they saw China as a unique place, a new frontier where they could have the sort of impact as an individual that would never be possible in the United States, as well as a role in establishing China as a great economic power. They tended to gravitate towards the commercial and financial hub of Shanghai rather than the ideological centre of Beijing. And it was in Shanghai in 2001 that Wendi Deng Murdoch found a new circle of well-heeled and well-connected US-educated Chinese friends, whose *guanxi* extended all the way to the top of the Chinese political hierarchy – albeit briefly.

Among those was Edward Tian, the founder of Asiainfo Holdings who became CEO of the state monopoly-breaking telecom company China Netcom. When he met Wendi, he was a 37-year-old former biology student from Beijing who had left China in 1987 to head for the US, where he earned a PhD in environmental management from Texas Tech University. On a trip back to China in 1991, Tian realised the enormous development that was taking place offered huge opportunities – but in telecommunications, not biology. In 1993 he joined a fellow overseas Chinese student in Texas, James Ding, to found Asiainfo Holdings, an internet infrastructure and software company. By 1995 Tian had moved the operations to China where, over the course of the next four years, he became a major player in the country's telecommunications sector. In 2000, having made a considerable fortune floating Asiainfo on the NASDAQ, Tian was invited to become President and CEO of China Netcom, the venture set up by the Chinese Academy of Science, SARFT, Shanghai Municipality and the Ministry of Railway, under the patronage of Jiang Mianheng, son of then-President Jiang Zemin. Tian and Wendi struck up a friendship and he was subsequently able to introduce Wendi to some of the key players in the Shanghai business network, which at the time was the most influential and powerful in the country. Through Tian, Wendi was able to broker relationships with Jiang Mianheng, which later led to the appointment of her husband to the China Netcom board. Tian, in turn, would later announce that Rupert Murdoch had become his 'hero and mentor'. Through the Shanghai connections she would also link up with Ding Yucheng, whose role in the Qinghai Satellite television deal proved both a boon and a bane to News Corp's China ambitions.

When I met with Wendi in Sydney for lunch at a waterfront restaurant in 2000, it was clear she was having little direct involvement in News Corp's business in China and was more than happy to be playing the role of homemaker. She was in the midst of renovating the Murdochs' newly acquired family apartment in New York's Soho district. She let slip that she was spending more on upgrading the home, a 2834 square-metre space that had been cobbled together on the top three floors of a former candy factory in a landmark building.

'I've been trying to do it myself,' she told me. 'But I keep on making mistakes and then we have to rip things out and start all over again. It's been so overwhelming, I just don't know what I'm doing.'

Wendi revealed that she had decided to get a designer in to take over the job. She said she had chosen Christian Liaigre, the French decorator responsible for the interiors at the nearby Mercer Hotel, where she and her husband had been renting a suite while the renovations were being carried out. Rupert Murdoch seemed intent on keeping his new wife busy as she no longer had any official role in the company business. Wendi said her husband had also asked her to oversee the redecorating of the other five homes they owned – in Los Angeles, London, Canberra and Carmel (California), plus the weekender at Centre Island, New York. The residences had previously been decorated under the tasteful eye of the former Mrs Murdoch, Anna.

During the lunch Wendi also let slip that she had recently been in Shanghai and had played a role in bringing 'MH' (as she referred to the Chinese President's son, Jiang Mianheng) to a deal with James and Rupert Murdoch. The reports that I was getting from my former colleagues at STAR TV were that while James sometimes welcomed the advice he received from his stepmother, he was also often annoyed by being second-guessed by his father back in New York, where the elder Murdoch was taking soundings from Wendi on a variety of China-related business issues. Rupert Murdoch had a habit of taking advice from a variety of sources – people who occupied positions above, around or below his own executives, even if those executives were his sons – and making up his own mind about how to proceed down a particular business path. James and Lachlan, I was told by a News Corp insider, often bridled at the interference in their decision making aided by the fact that their stepmother was the last one to have their father's ear at the end of each working day.

But as Wendi indicated at the lunch, she had things on her mind other than business in China. In November 2001 she gave birth to a daughter, Grace Helen Murdoch, who was joined by a sister, Chloe Murdoch, just under two years later in July 2003. The arrival of two more children into the Murdoch dynasty did nothing to clarify the lines of succession at News Corp. Wendi wasted no time, however, in ensuring that her daughters grew up well aware not just of their Murdoch heritage but of their Chinese roots as well. She hired Mandarin-speaking nannies so that the children would be bilingual and bicultural from infancy – a fact that would later irritate the older Murdoch, who has often complained he cannot understand the conversations between mother and daughters being conducted in his own family living room.

By all accounts Wendi remained largely preoccupied with motherhood during this period. The executives at STAR said it was clear Murdoch continued to consult closely with his wife on matters relating to China but he was also taking advice from a range of people. In relation to the disastrous Qinghai Satellite television deal, which would eventually provide a major setback for Murdoch's ambitions in China, they said Wendi was one of those convinced that Ding Yucheng had the necessary high-level backing to deliver on the project – despite the reservations of some other News Corp executives in China.

Wendi accompanied her husband to Beijing in March 2005, just six months before Murdoch's 'hitting the wall' remarks that followed the government's annulment of the Qinghai Satellite deal. But her motives were other than business. She was hunting for another home, this time in downtown Beijing. She had her mind set on a traditional courtyard-style house in Beijing's exclusive Beichizi district, a block from the Forbidden City. Perhaps fittingly, the house, with its steep-pitched roofs and wooden eaves of vermilion and gold, had reportedly once been the home of one the most powerful Mandarins to have served the Chinese emperor's court. Wendi was determined not just to preserve a piece of Beijing's heritage for her daughters, but also to send a signal about her own commitment to China in the future.

Her chance came with the News Corp purchase of Intermix Media, owner of MySpace.com – the fifth most-viewed internet domain in the US – for US$580 million in July 2005. MySpace is a social networking site where users can put up information about themselves for dating, making friends, professional networking and sharing interests. In September 2006, Murdoch announced plans to expand MySpace internationally – including China.

'We have to make MySpace a very Chinese site,' Murdoch said at a media conference organised by merchant banker Goldman Sachs in New York. 'I have sent my wife across there because she understands the language.'

Up until then, Wendi had held no official position within News Corp other than that of unofficial adviser to her husband. MySpace China would give her the opportunity to show off her business acumen and prove to her detractors that she was something other than an attractive appendage to an ageing billionaire media mogul.

The role suited her because it involved 'new media', the sector her generation had grown up with and which she believed she understood better than nearly every other person in the extended Murdoch family, with the possible exception of James. It also was about China – the one area where she could at least claim a degree of cultural insider's knowledge, which meant she would likely be left to run the show on her own. As Wendi told me back in the Sydney restaurant five years previously, she had no long-term intention of being 'a stay-at-home society wife'. She has a point to prove.

In any future divvy-up of the News Corp empire that would follow the death of the patriarch, Wendi Deng Murdoch would be intent on ensuring that she has carved out her niche. To date, all the other likely heirs – Lachlan, James, Elisabeth and Prudence (via her husband Alasdair MacLeod) – have all held senior management positions within News Corp and, at the very least, demonstrated a capacity for management. Wendi needs to make her mark and state her credentials.

Wendi demonstrated a far more considered approach to the MySpace China launch than would have been expected had it remained under the direct influence of her husband. She made frequent trips to China during late 2006 to lay the political and business groundwork. Rather than have News Corp attempt to exert its control over all of MySpace China she effectively brought in a range of partners with demonstrated success in the China market to help run the show. The partners include her old friend

Edward Tian, whose new investment company China Broadband Capital Partners holds a stake in MySpace China and a seat on the board. The strategy devised by Wendi was to effectively license the MySpace brand and have local Chinese entrepreneurs establish and build the business in a way acceptable to the Chinese market. She also hired Luo Chuan, a former head of Microsoft's MSN internet service in China, to run the operation. In a sign of her commitment to the new venture, in July 2007 News Corp announced that Wendi Deng Murdoch had been appointed to the position of Chief of Strategy for MySpace China's operation. It is her first official role inside the family company since marrying Murdoch.

It is a prominent role in a market where there are already a number of established domestic players and where her profile will ensure that her success or failure will remain firmly in the public spotlight. But it will also be the opportunity for her to showcase the very same traits she shares with her spouse – a pragmatic, single-minded determination to prove the naysayers wrong and to make the most of every opportunity. She has the goods to make it work – and, of course, access to some very deep pockets.

To the outside world, Wendi Deng Murdoch still has a great deal to prove. Her husband's detractors would have it that she is little more than the 'trophy wife' of a wealthy septuagenarian, while the conspirators have long been convinced she is a Chinese spy. She has been labelled both a gold-digger desirous of her husband's fortune and Murdoch's key to the potential riches of the Chinese media market. The truth is that she is none of the above.

Kathy Freston, addressing the crowd at the Core Club, said finding 'the One' was about falling in love and being 'drawn into something bigger than ourselves, as if we are being called upon to participate in something important unfolding within and all around us'. As her book expounds, 'When love is in the air, we find ourselves at the centre of the universe with all the wheels of creation in full motion.'

Wendi's relationship with Murdoch has no doubt led her to the centre of a new universe far from her roots in provincial China. She was so taken by the author's approach to achieving soul-mate love via vegetarianism, yoga, prayer and devotion that in early 2007 she, Freston and three other girlfriends spent a week aboard the new Murdoch family yacht *Rosehearty* in the Caribbean, studying and practising the principles espoused in Freston's *Finding the One*.

'She corrupted us!' Wendi told *The New Yorker*. 'Vegetarian food, no drinking, no leather. She said we had to wear Payless shoes!'

So who is Wendi Deng? It may be that she is indeed Rupert Murdoch's 'One'. But she has yet to prove she is also 'the One' who holds the key to China.

22

The End of the Affair

After a decade and a half of trying, Rupert Murdoch's attempted seduction of China has ended in a case of unrequited love. The world's most powerful media baron is the spurned suitor left standing at the palace gates of the Middle Kingdom waiting for someone to let him in. No one has been more relentless in wooing the ruling elite. No one has risked more financially nor put as much of their own personal prestige at stake. Yet he remains there on the portico, flowers in hand, all dressed up but nowhere to go.

Certainly Murdoch is at the front of a long line of potential rivals seeking entry to China's 380 million television homes, and should the door ever open he will undoubtedly be the first through the entrance. It is a position he occupies by dint of the extraordinary pragmatism he brings into play. In China, Murdoch's detractors would argue he has put potential profit before principle in his attempts to inveigle the Beijing leadership and win their trust and confidence. It is rare that the tycoon's legendary charm and persuasive powers are rebuffed by the targets of his affections. But Murdoch was so ardent, so zealous, in his desire for a piece of the China market that he ended up estranging himself from China's ruling elite.

There are now signs that both Murdoch's patience and ardour for China are waning. In June 2006 he sold off half of his remaining interest in Phoenix Television to mobile telephone operator China Mobile. In February 2007 Murdoch again reshuffled the executives at STAR, replacing Michelle Guthrie with former merchant banker Paul Aiello, who had joined the company just a year earlier as President. The company also moved to cut back its local production ventures in China and talk down the prospects of its Xing Kong channel. At a media analysts' briefing in the northern spring of 2007 Murdoch was proffering a far more circumspect picture of the China market.

'We don't do very well in China. We have an interest. We just sold half of it in Phoenix Television . . . We have got five times our money back of our total investment and we are still there. We brought on a new partner, China Mobile, and this has been a very good base and we think it will do nicely. And we have our own little channel, Xing Kong, which is produced in Shanghai and distributed through the southeast. That's pretty much a break-even operation,' he said.

'We are very modest. All I would say there is that nobody – and

I challenge anyone to argue this – nobody, none of the American media companies or British media companies have made any impact there yet. There may be a MySpace China which has been licensed but we are just feeling our way there . . . It's a vast market, but it's certainly a very, very sensitive one . . . It is a very difficult market for outsiders.'

While the results of Murdoch's unashamed courting of China might be construed as a failure, the process in itself did much to revolutionise the Chinese media sector. As in virtually every country in which the media baron has operated, Murdoch has been an extraordinary catalyst of change in China. In the same way he took on the Fleet Street unions and turned the British newspaper printing business on its head, and launched satellite television in the UK and established the Fox Cable network in the US, Murdoch's coming to China galvanised the Beijing leadership and set in train a transformation of its formerly staid, conservative media sector.

When the Politburo conservatives were about to pull down the shutters on the internet phenomenon, Murdoch's tacit assistance towards putting *People's Daily* online opened the eyes of the ruling elite old guard to the potential of the newfangled World Wide Web. Instead of it being curtailed, it spread. The Chinese people were encouraged to embrace the internet and despite various attempts by the authorities to restrict or censor its content since, it is a free-flowing tap of information that can never be totally turned off or controlled.

The advent of the Phoenix Chinese Channel provided an enormous catalyst for change in China's television industry. Because it was a general entertainment Mandarin-language channel it presented Chinese viewers for the first time with a true comparison to the dour programming of the national broadcaster, CCTV. It astounded its audience – limited as it was but highly influential – with innovative programming, computer-generated graphics and slick presentation skills. It introduced viewers to Western-style news and current affairs formats with a bevy of telegenic female journalists and male newsreaders, who were actually out in the field asking questions rather than stoically reciting statistics of rice production from behind a desk in front of a grey studio set. When then-Premier Zhu Rongji announced at a press conference in 1998 that Phoenix had become his favourite television channel he was speaking on behalf of a much larger audience. Within a year CCTV had invested tens of millions of dollars in new production equipment and studios and began emulating Phoenix with a host of new news and current affairs shows, which were in turn cloned by every provincial television station in the country.

The Xing Kong Wei Shi channel launch, with its diet of variety, talk and reality programming, likewise turned the China broadcasting industry on its head. Few apart from Murdoch would have had the fortitude to commit to the extraordinary financial investment required to produce some seventeen original shows, totalling more than 700 hours of television, in the channel's first year of operation.

It might well have been lowbrow, populist programming modelled on the success of the Fox Cable network in the US, but it proved the Chinese television audience's taste was little different from that of the Western world. Where Phoenix started a trend in popular television programming, Xing Kong was pure Murdoch brilliance, targeting China's new generation of eighteen- to 35-year-olds with a mixture of brash, innovative tabloid television. Much of it may have been branded 'vulgar and degrading' by the Beijing authorities, but nonetheless it soon became a programming mainstay of Chinese viewers across the country.

The great irony for Murdoch is that having played so significant a part in the opening up of China's media sector, he is still largely confined to the outside, looking in. All the while, his perceived transgressions in China were starting to be a crucial factor in his other business dealings around the world. The media tycoon's audacious and ultimately successful US$5 billion bid for the Dow Jones company and *The Wall Street Journal* newspaper in 2007 was initially opposed by both key shareholders and staff partly on the basis of Murdoch's apparent kowtowing to the Chinese authorities in order to further his business interests there.

James H Ottaway, a key shareholder in Dow Jones, issued a statement soon after Murdoch made his bid for the company public in May, stating that 'Dow Jones is not for sale, at any price, to Rupert Murdoch'. He accused Murdoch of caving in to political pressure to advance his business interests, contrasting the actions of News Corp company STAR in bowing to Chinese government censorship, with the *Journal*'s editorial page censure of Chinese human rights abuses. 'I doubt its freedom to criticise the Chinese government would continue under Murdoch ownership,' he said. News Corp dismissed the accusations by Ottaway as being based on tired misconceptions and clichés.

The Wall Street Journal's China-based journalists also opposed the bid, with seven signing a letter in which they said they feared that 'News Corp's acquisition of Dow Jones would threaten the paper's integrity, credibility and high journalistic standards'. Most of the paper's China staff signed the letter, including members of the team that won the Pulitzer Prize for international reporting in 2007 for a largely critical examination of the consequences of China's rapid economic growth.

'News Corporation Chairman Rupert Murdoch has a well-documented history of making editorial decisions in order to advance his business interests in China, and indeed, of sacrificing journalistic integrity to satisfy personal and political aims,' the letter stated.

In truth, neither the signatories, *The Wall Street Journal* itself, nor *The New York Times*, which ran long investigative articles in relation to Murdoch's activities in China, were able to cite a single incident of the media proprietor interfering in his company's media coverage of China – apart from the quashing by HarperCollins of the Chris Patten book.

Indeed, had Murdoch's attempted seduction of Beijing been

more successful and his business interests better placed than they currently are, it is doubtful whether the media tycoon would have proceeded with his bid for *The Wall Street Journal*. The newspaper provides the best, most comprehensive and objective reporting and analysis of events in China – often to the chagrin of the nation's political and business leaders. If Murdoch was still sitting down to intimate private dinners at Zhongnanhai with the ruling elite as he had in the past, it is difficult imagining him explaining away the *Journal*'s often aggressive, critical coverage, or that he as Dow Jones proprietor could do little or nothing about it. It is doubtful whether Murdoch would be able to hold both in his hand – a successful Chinese business empire, which requires a certain amount of acquiescence to the wishes of its rulers, and a newspaper which places its journalistic integrity above all else, including its own business interests. That Murdoch agreed to uphold and protect the *Journal*'s independence is probably the best indication yet that he has tired of China; that his passion for its potential riches has dwindled and that he is moving on to his next big adventure.

India, rather than China, has become the new focus of Murdoch's attentions. At the McGraw-Hill Media Summit in February 2007, the media tycoon pronounced that India was now the 'most exciting among developing countries for media'. He noted that even though India was behind China in terms of market development, 'the political and social vibrancy of the country, and the zeal of Indians, make it one of the most attractive destinations for investments'. China was fast sliding down his list of priorities. India is a working democracy and Murdoch has always felt more at home in a system where his media power and economic clout amounted to political influence. The Beijing ruling elite, unaffected by public opinion and not subject to election by the masses, could afford to spurn the mogul's overtures.

Murdoch could simply bide his time, waiting for the Chinese leadership to open its door to the foreign media. But conservative President Hu Jintao shows little sign of relaxing the iron-fisted controls he and his minions have reasserted over the country's media. Hu is just halfway through an expected ten-year term as leader. Even if there is a generational change at that time, resulting in a Chinese leadership more comfortable with the advent of Western influence on the nation's media sector, Murdoch will by then be eighty-one years old and it's doubtful he will still possess the same verve for China that he has had in the past.

And News Corp's next generation? Of the Murdoch dynasty, no one apart from Wendi shows any interest in carrying the family standard to China. Lachlan Murdoch, starting to feel like the business equivalent of Prince Charles, forever waiting for his parent to abdicate so he could take a shot at the top job, resigned from all executive roles at News Corporation in July 2005, citing the need 'to do his own thing'. Since then he has exhibited no interest in the market his father pursued so persistently, preferring instead to seek out opportunities via his private company, Illyria Pty Ltd, in

Australia and India. James Murdoch, who spent three and a half years at the helm of STAR, is said to have enjoyed his time there but only ever saw it as a stepping stone to a bigger role at BSkyB – in the market of a Western democracy where he understands the language, the culture and the political dynamics. In the event of any future carve-up of the empire, it is James who will most likely step into the shoes of his father, but his attention will be on the continued transformation of an old media company into a new media one. Murdoch's oldest daughters Prudence and Elisabeth seem content in London and Sydney respectively, and have shown little indication of wanting to re-enter the family business, let alone take on the China market.

Even within News Corp itself, China has long been the personal domain of Rupert, with few of his other senior executives ever dipping theirs toes in the market. The corporation's Chief Operating Officer, Peter Chernin, although recently stepping up his profile in India, has rarely intervened in the China operations.

Which leaves Wendi and the couple's Chinese-American daughters, Grace and Chloe, whose heritage ensures some vested interest in China. In the future, the emerging economic powerhouses of China and India could well hold the key to the survival of global transnationals such as News Corporation. There would be a certain irony should it eventuate that having set out to conquer the Middle Kingdom, Murdoch ends up with his company's future beholden to China, and in the hands of his Chinese-born wife.

But Wendi will find a media market far different from that envisaged by her husband when he first ventured into China fifteen years earlier. The Beijing leadership, by effectively out-manoeuvring Murdoch and keeping him at bay for such a period, have bought time for the nation's own media to mature and develop. China's myriad television broadcasters have evolved, merging, modernising and cloning themselves into powerful, financially strong corporations which will prove no easy pushover for the big Western media companies, which once thought they could simply bankroll their way to dominance. The Chinese are fiercely nationalistic and will fight to protect their domestic market from 'foreign invaders'.

And even if Beijing does ease open the gates, News Corp may well have missed their chance at the main game, only to find themselves left to sweep up the crumbs. Such is the case already for Wendi and her struggle to establish MySpace China in an internet market already dominated by local businesses such as 51.com, Baidu and Tencent, and myriad other social networking sites such as Tudou.com and Rox.com.cn. At the time of writing, reports suggest MySpace has an estimated 600 000 registered users, while 51.com claims 60 million accounts and growth of five million new accounts per month. As with satellite television, Chinese entrepreneurs have emulated the successes of the social networking phenomenon, particularly the Murdoch-owned MySpace, and reaped the rewards.

The world's most powerful media mogul's time in China may well have come and gone. The Chinese leadership appears to have strategically outlasted him, thereby successfully seeing off the 'unambiguous threat' of new telecommunications technologies which Murdoch fatefully championed. His experience in China has been particularly galling for a tycoon whose relentless pragmatism has meant he has rarely had to acknowledge defeat in pursuit of a business deal. He has built an empire on an ability to peer into the future and see opportunities on the media landscape that his rivals cannot – or if they can, they are too timid to exploit them. Murdoch saw the potential of the China television market even though it remained largely closed to the Western media. He remained convinced that in the same way that he had challenged the status quo in Australia, Britain and the US, his influence, money and charm would enable him to gain access to the living rooms of China. Political leaders the world over have fallen under the Murdoch spell, and for a while it seemed as though the media mogul would have his wanton ways in China as well. But in seeking to woo the Chinese leadership, Murdoch overstepped the mark – he became too impetuous, too impudent. The affair, and the adventure, has come to an end.

Withdrawn from
Lambeth Libraries

Index